DESPERATE
Moments

40-DAY JOURNEY
THROUGH THE LIVES OF HANNAH, JONAH, AND RUTH

CLARA HANNAH

Bible Copyright

Scripture quotations marked (NASB) are taken from the New American Standard Bible®, Copyright © 1960, 1971, 1977, 1995, 2020 by The Lockman Foundation. Used by permission. All rights reserved. lockman.org

Scripture quotations marked (AMP) are taken from the Amplified Bible, Copyright © 2015 by The Lockman Foundation. Used by permission.

Scripture quotations marked (NIV) are taken from the Holy Bible, New International Version®, NIV®. Copyright © 1973, 1978, 1984, 2011 by Biblica, Inc.™ Used by permission of Zondervan. All rights reserved worldwide. www.zondervan.com The "NIV" and "New International Version" are trademarks registered in the United States Patent and Trademark Office by Biblica, Inc.™

"Scripture quotations marked (ESV) are from The ESV® Bible (The Holy Bible, English Standard Version®), © 2001 by Crossway, a publishing ministry of Good News Publishers. Used by permission. All rights reserved."

Scripture quotations marked (NKJV) are from the New King James Version®. Copyright © 1982 by Thomas Nelson. Used by permission. All rights reserved.

Contents

Foreword 1
Acknowledgments 3
Dedication 5
Introduction 6
A Life "Preflight Checklist" 8
Goals of this Book 10
How to Get Started 11

CHAPTER 1:
HANNAH: FROM HUMBLED TO HONORED 12

Day One 13
    Background on Hannah and the Nation of Israel 13
    Life Lesson #1: Learning from the Past 16

Day Two 19
    Hannah's Hardship 19
    Women in Ancient Israel 19
    Life Lesson # 2: We Need One Another 21
    Personal Story: God's Family Right on Time 22

Day Three 25
    Elkanah's Solution to Hannah's Problem (1 Samuel 1:1-2) 25
    Life Lesson #3: God's Ways vs. Culture 26

Day Four 31
    Hannah's Desperate Moment (1 Samuel 1:3-8) 31

    Life Lesson # 4: Do Not Seek in People
    What Only God Can Do for You..................................33

Day Five 38
    Hannah Took Action (1 Samuel 1:9) 38
    Life Lesson # 5: Don't Look Around You....................39

Day Six..43
    Hannah's Desperate Prayer (1 Samuel 1:10-12).......43
    Life Lesson # 6: Spontaneous vs. Distant Prayer....................45

Day Seven 50
    Hannah's Servant's Heart 50
    Life Lesson # 7: More Than What's Required........................51

Day Eight..54
    The Priest Misinterpreted Hannah (1 Samuel 1:13-16) 54
    Life Lesson # 8: Surrendering our Reputation....................55
    Personal Story: Persisting Amidst Opposition....................57

Day Nine 62
    Hannah received a Word from God (1 Samuel 1:17-19) 62
    Hannah's Miracle: More Than She Asked For!
    (1 Samuel 1:20 and 2:21)..63
    Life Lesson # 9: In Due Season 64
    Personal Story: The Natural Waiting Period 65

Day Ten..68
    Hannah Fulfills Her Promise to God (1 Samuel 1:21-23).......68
    Life Lesson # 10: Obedience vs. Sacrifices 69
    Personal Story: Sowing My Accomplishments 70

Day Eleven 73
    Hannah's Offering (1 Samuel 1:24-28) 73
    Life Lesson # 11: Heart Worship vs Lip Service 74
    Personal Story: Dating 75

Day Twelve 78
    Hannah's Grateful Heart (1 Samuel 2:1-10) 78
    Life Lesson # 12: Gratitude Before the Breakthrough 80
    Personal Story: Perspective 81

Day Thirteen 84
    Hannah's Legacy 84
    Life Lesson # 13: God Chooses the
    "Least Likely to Succeed" 85

Day Fourteen 93
    Main Takeaways from Hannah's Life 93

CHAPTER 2:
JONAH: FROM FUGITIVE TO FAITHFUL 98

Day Fifteen 99
    Background on Jonah and the Nation of Israel 99
    Life Lesson # 15: Remain Humble in Prosperity 100

Day Sixteen 105
    Jonah Received an Assignment from God (Jonah 1:1-2) 105
    Why Did Jonah Run Away? 106
    Israel-Assyria Conflict 107
    Life Lesson # 16: Disobedience: An Open Door 108

Day Seventeen ... 113
Why Did Jonah Disobey? ... 113
Life Lesson # 17: Social Constructs Above God's Direction ... 115

Day Eighteen ... 120
Jonah's Journey Away from His Calling (Jonah 1:4-16) ... 120
Life Lesson # 18: Being Real but Improper vs. Fake and Proper ... 123

Day Nineteen ... 128
Jonah's Desperate Moment (Jonah 1:17-2:9) ... 128
Jonah's Desperate Cry ... 128
Jonah's Immediate Answer to Prayer ... 129
Life Lesson # 19: We Have the Answer as Soon as We Ask ... 132

Day Twenty ... 135
Jonah's Miracle (Jonah 2:10) ... 135
Personal Story: God Brought Me back to the United States Against All Odds ... 135
Jonah's Second Chance (Jonah 3:1-3) ... 137
Life Lesson #20: God Makes a Way ... 138

Day Twenty-one ... 141
Jonah's Message and Nineveh's Response (Jonah 3:4-10) ... 141
Background on Assyria ... 141
God Orchestrated the Universe for This Very Moment ... 143
Life Lesson # 21: An Entire Nation Can Be Saved ... 145
Personal Story: What Motivates You? ... 148

Day Twenty-two ... 152
Two Groups of People That Needed God's Mercy ... 152
Life Lesson # 22: God Doesn't Play Favorites ... 152

Personal Story: Pastor Opened Up to Change 155

Day Twenty-three 161
    God Restored Nineveh (3:10-4:11) 161
    Why Was Jonah So Angry? 162
    Life Lesson # 23: Be Real with God 162
    Personal Story: Learning to be Authentic 165

Day Twenty-four 170
    The Root of Jonah's Frustration 170
    Life Lesson # 24: That Thing That Aggravates
    You is There by Design 170
    Personal Story: God Dealt with
    My Pride Through This Assignment 171

Day Twenty-five 175
    Ninevah Was Spared, But Not Forever 175
    Jonah Was a Picture of Jesus 176
    Life Lesson # 25: Love for "Outsiders" and Forgiveness 177

Day Twenty-six 182
    Main Takeaways from the Life of Jonah 182

CHAPTER 3:
RUTH: FROM OUTCAST TO ROYALTY 186

Day Twenty-seven 187
    Introduction (Ruth1:1) 187
    Background on Famines 188
    Elimelech's Desperate Moment (Ruth 1:2) 189
    Elimelech was a Fool 190
    Life Lesson # 27: The Danger of Making Rash Decisions ... 191

Personal Story: Follow Peace 193

Day Twenty-eight 198
    Stepping Out of God's Will 198
    More Wrong Choices 198
    Life Lesson # 28: Consulting
    the Lord Before Every Decision 200
    Personal Story: Choosing the Right School 200

Day Twenty-nine 205
    Elimelech's Legacy 205
    Widows in Ancient Israel 205
    Naomi Took Action in the Midst of
    Her Desperate Moment (Ruth 1:6) 206
    Life Lesson # 29: Faith Plus Action 207

Day Thirty 210
    Naomi Returns to God 210
    Ruth and Orpa Follow Naomi (Ruth 1:10-14) 210
    Life Lesson # 30: Everything Must Bow Down to God 213
    Personal Story: Busy Season Was Not an Excuse 214
    Personal Story: Times of Preparation 216

Day Thirty-one 219
    Ruth Commits Her Life Fully to God (Ruth 1:16-18) 219
    Life Lesson # 31: The Lord Cares for
    the Oppressed in Society 220

Day Thirty-two 225
    The Journey to Bethlehem: It Took Action (Ruth 1:19-22) ... 225
    Life Lesson # 32: Don't Reference
    the Past—He is Doing Something New 226

Day Thirty-three 230
   Proof of Repentance 230
   Life Lesson #33: God Rewards Obedience, Not Perfection 230

Day Thirty-four 233
   The Process Before the Miracle (Ruth 2:1-9) 233
   Life Lesson # 34: Don't Give Up; It's a Process 235

Day Thirty-five 241
   Interaction Between Ruth and Boaz (Ruth 2:10-16) 241
   Life Lesson # 35: Expect Far More Than You Asked For 242

Day Thirty-six 247
   Ruth Shares the News with Naomi (Ruth 2:17-23) 247
   Life Lesson # 36: God's Blessings are Comprehensive 248

Day Thirty-seven 253
   Ruth and Naomi Move in Faith (Ruth 3:1-18) 253
   Life Lesson # 37: Patiently Waiting vs. Passively Waiting 256
   Personal Story: Waiting to Meet My Husband 259

Day Thirty-eight 263
   The Decision That Changed Everything (Ruth 4:1-12) 263
   Life Lesson #38: The Value of "Spoken Blessings" 265
   Personal Story: Calling Things That Are Not as If They Were .. 268

Day Thirty-nine 272
   The Ultimate Miracle (Ruth 4:13-22) 272
   The Lineage of King David 273
   Life Lesson #39: We Were Created with an Eternal Purpose ... 274

Day Forty 277
   Main Takeaways from the Life of Ruth 277

CONCLUSION 281
    The Power of a Desperate Situation 281
    The Most Desperate Moment Anyone Could Face 282
    Salvation/Rededication Prayer 285
    Welcome to the Family of God! 286
    The Power to Live a Life of Victory 286
    Personal Story: The Baptism of
    the Holy Spirit When I was 15 289
    Baptism of the Holy Spirit Prayer 291

END NOTES 293
    Chapter 1: Hannah 293
    Chapter 2: Jonah 295
    Chapter 3: Ruth 297

Foreword

It is my pleasure to have the privilege to speak enthusiastically on behalf of Clara Hannah and her first—but hopefully not last—book. Clara is not only a dear sister in Christ but also a sister of sorts in the flesh by virtue of her marriage to John Hannah, my nephew, whom I had the honor of leading to a saving knowledge of Jesus Christ at the age of 10.

Clara has done a masterful job in composing this Bible Study + Devotional; it reflects her diligence and resonates her passion as a Christian Teacher who seeks to edify the Reader, through sound Theological Research together with a personal application grounded in her own "Desperate Moments." Using the life stories of three prominent Biblical characters (Hannah, Jonah and Ruth) as Scriptural precedence, she artfully and thoroughly walks you through a '40-Day wilderness journey' that encompasses Background, Historical context, Bible verses, Life Lessons, Questions to Reflect on, and Breakthrough Prayer. Be sure to also take to take to heart her exhortation to receive the Baptism in the Holy Spirit.

She may be a Novice as a Christian Author in this -her first literary endeavor- but her commitment and dedication to Jesus Christ, her savior and Lord, is genuine and without question. You can sense this character quality as you embark on this journey with her. She was born in Argentina and raised by Godly Christian parents. I have observed her spiritual walk with the Lord as a Christian sister, a loving Christian wife, a devoted Christian mother of three young children, a homemaker, a homeschool teacher, a Christian worker, and a servant in her local church, and now as a Theologically-trained Teacher of God's Word.

Clara's recent Master's degree in Biblical Exposition from Liberty University attests to her competence and credentials in 'rightly dividing the Word of truth' (2nd Timothy 2:15) to earn the Reader's attention and demonstrate her credibility. In short, Clara Hannah, by the grace of God and the empowerment of the Holy Spirit -with all she has on her plate- is worthy of respect as an anointed servant of the Lord.

Given my own ministerial background and experience as a Seminary Graduate (Master of Divinity), as a Missionary to Jewish People for twenty years in the Brooklyn/New York Metro area, and as an Itinerant Evangelist/Preacher/Teacher locally, nationally, and internationally, I can vouch to the quality to Clara's Theological acumen and her ability to connect with fellow Christians. My numerous conversations and prayer times with her have augmented my conviction in this regard.

I encourage you to take this 40-day Journey with Clara Hannah. It will prove to be an exciting and worthwhile Spiritual expedition for women, as well as for us men. It is intended for all Christians who have been in near-hopeless situations in life (and haven't we all?). Clara will help you to know with assurance that no situation is hopeless with God and lead you to that glorious place of 'SURRENDER' to Jesus Christ and His plans and purposes for your life (Jeremiah 29:11-13).

You will proclaim, as I often say to Clara, 'Gloria a Dios!

Don Geraci
Holbrook, New York

Acknowledgments

I would like to acknowledge first and foremost the Holy Spirit of God, who has helped me not only write this book but also most importantly has been there to help me in every "Desperate Moment" in my life. He has been my guide, my strength, my counselor, my refuge, my encourager, and "my ever-present help in times of need."

I also want to thank God the Father for his protection, provision, wisdom, and victory in every battle, and Jesus Christ, my Savior, who died in my place. It is through His obedience and sacrifice on the cross that I am able to access the throne of God and have communion with the Holy Spirit every day.

I would also like to acknowledge my dad, Manuel Gonzalez Dorado, who led me to Christ, at an early age and also modeled serving Christ and being bold for his faith, even when it was not the popular thing to do. He always believed in me and encouraged me to pursue my dreams. His words of encouragement are continually before me.

I'd like to thank God for my twin sister, Ana Ines Rodriguez, who has always been by my side. It is alongside her that I have learned some of the finest lessons of faith and trust in God. She has been with me through the ups and downs of life. We received the Baptism of the Holy Spirit together at the age of 15 and both decided to follow the call of God in our lives. We moved to the United States at 19, trusting and believing God at every step. She has been one of the greatest gifts of God in my life.

I'm also very thankful for my mom, Lea Buono, for allowing my sister and I to follow God's plans for our lives, even when they were unconventional, and for her support throughout the years.

I'd also like to recognize some amazing people that the Lord has placed in my path through the years, who have helped me during some of the hardest times of my life, without expecting anything in return:

My aunt and uncle Jorge and Teresita Olea provided us with a place to stay many times during our college years and a loving family environment, as well as a wonderful example of being true servants of Christ on and off the pulpit.

Liz Wernz, helped me get my Driver's license and cooked the best Thanksgiving meals for me and all the other International Students at Northern Kentucky University, giving us a family far away from home.

Britt and Melissa Moss, who felt led by the Lord to allow me to live in their home during my time at the University of Louisiana at Monroe. They not only provided me with a place to stay, they became my family.

My grandmother, Zulema San Pedro, who taught me to be tough and gave me food to put in my luggage when I moved to Buenos Aires.

Uncle Don Geraci for his encouragement, wisdom and prayers that allowed me to carry on and finish this assignment.

Finally, I would like to thank my husband, John Hannah, for believing in me and being patient while I figured out what exactly God wanted me to do, and has been there for me during the entire process.

Dedication

I dedicate this book to our three amazing children: Dylan, Daniella and Delfina. They bring so much joy and purpose to our lives! I pray that this book, but most importantly my everyday life, will be a testimony to them of God's love and faithfulness, as well as a tangible example of what stepping out in Faith looks like.

Introduction

When I began writing this book, my intention was to showcase people in the Bible who had gone through "Desperate Moments" and whose lives were turned around with the help of God. I wanted to inspire people from all walks of life turn to God with the confidence that He can take the most hopeless circumstance and turn that into a Legacy. Because that is the kind of God He is.

Even though that is definitely a major part of the message of this book, as I started studying the lives of these heroes of the faith, who in all honesty were just like you and me, I realized their lives were complex, and their stories were written in the Bible with much detail and rich context for a reason.

God intended for us to savor each verse and, in doing so, find the hidden treasures and life lessons that we would otherwise miss. 2 Timothy 3:16-17 (NASB) states:

> *"All Scripture is inspired by God and beneficial for teaching, for rebuke, for correction, for training in righteousness; so that the man or woman of God may be fully capable, equipped for every good work."*

When we realize that even the details of each story are meant for our training, we develop the hunger and thirst to decipher what they mean. As we dig deeper into them, we will learn more about these characters, get to know God more intimately, and understand who He is, what He values in people, and how He operates. There is a reason why these stories were placed in God's Holy Word.

My intention now, besides the encouragement, is to share what I've discovered about these stories and how those life lessons can be applied to us today. Dare to be surprised and open up your heart to what God has in store for you; it might not be what you are expecting!

A Life "Preflight Checklist"

Forty days of delving into the stories of these Bible individuals will serve as a two-fold blessing. On one hand, it will provide knowledge and a deeper understanding of some of the hidden lessons of these well-known stories. On the other hand, it serves as a "checklist" to help us ensure our lives reflect God's principles and are headed in the right direction.

A pilot's pre-flight checklist is a "list of tasks that the pilot or the flight crew must perform before takeoff" and "It covers the steps and safety checks to ensure the aircraft is ready to fly." My husband has been an airline pilot for almost 20 years. Although he has performed thousands of successful flights throughout his career, he must follow the checklist each time. Every flight of his career has been successful, but not every item was checked off immediately. On numerous occasions while following the checklist, he was able to notice issues that needed attention. Sometimes, this meant calling the dispatcher, maintenance, or customer operations to review the problem further, which may have turned into a delay. If something was not up to the safety standard, it needed to be addressed immediately. This was a temporary inconvenience for the passengers, the crew members, and many others counting on that flight to leave on schedule. Still, it was worth it in the end, as every flight took off and landed successfully.

When it comes to our lives, it's essential that we also follow a "pre-flight checklist" regularly if we desire to "take off and land the airplane" of our lives successfully once we leave this earth. These "life safety standards" were put in place by our Heavenly Father in the Bible to help us in the journey of life. Hebrews 4:12 (NASB) states:

> *"For the word of God is living and active, and sharper than any two-edged sword, even penetrating as far as the division of soul and spirit, of both joints and marrow, and able to judge the thoughts and intentions of the heart."*

Just like my husband, who still needs to check the aircraft before every flight, even though he has been flying for almost two decades, it does not matter how long we have been following God, whether it's been a week, an hour, or many years, we must always go back to His Word. This will ensure we continue the course and finish strong. 1 Corinthians 1:18-19 (NASB) states:

> *"For the word of the cross is foolishness to those who are perishing, but to us who are being saved it is the power of God. For it is written: "I will destroy the wisdom of the wise, and the understanding of those who have understanding, I will confound."*

Many might argue that to base our lives on the Word of God is nonsense, but this is only because they have not experienced its life-changing power yet. The wisdom of God surpasses the wisdom of this world, and if we follow Him, we will experience a journey that we never thought possible.

Goals of this Book

The main goal of this Book is to encourage anyone going through a "Desperate Moment" by pointing out people in the Bible in similar situations who were able to experience significant breakthroughs by placing their trust in God.

Another, equally important goal, is to bring us back to appreciating the real-life stories of the Bible. They were set in place by God, so that we could learn from their complex set of circumstances and apply this wisdom into our own lives today. The Word of God was meant, not as a Historical account alone, but most importantly to bring guidance, encouragement and abundant life to those who read it and take it to heart!

How to Get Started

This 40-day journey can be treated as a daily personal or family Bible Study. It contains a unique Life lesson and Questions to reflect at the end of each day, which are helpful and can be used as a daily devotional.

Another practical approach would be to study it with a group. If each person completes five "Days" a week at home, they can meet up weekly for discussion and prayer. Under this format this entire Bible Study would be completed in eight weeks.

This format is meant to lead you deeper into the Scriptures. Even though each day has a unique message, they build on each other. As you get further into the stories, you will find yourself going deeper and deeper into the Word of God, which is the one true secret to any real, lasting breakthrough!

It's important to note that the daily 'Life Lessons' are not magic formulas that work in a void. Every aspect of our lives is interconnected. If one area is out of line with God's will, it affects all others.

Hannah, Jonah, and Ruth's breakthroughs were journeys that started way before the 'breakthrough moment.' God was molding their hearts to be ready for that time. Their hearts underwent a progressive transformation, leaving them ready to receive what God had in store. They were being set free from traditions, culture, prejudices, fears, wrong mindsets or other hindrances that would otherwise have stopped them from receiving what God had planned for their lives. I pray this will become your own "journey of transformation," where you open your heart to God and all that He desires to speak to you, so that you can also receive all that He has planned for your life!

Chapter 1:

Hannah: From Humbled to Honored

Days 1-14

Day One

Background on Hannah and the Nation of Israel

Hannah's story is narrated in a few short chapters, but the repercussions of her faith, actions, and loyalty to God extend throughout the Bible, even to the birth of Jesus and beyond.

Hannah lived in Israel around 1150 B.C. (the early Iron Age)[1] in a town known as Ramah, about five miles north of Jerusalem. She lived in a region known as the "central highlands" west of the Mediterranean Sea. This region is where the Israelites settled after the Exodus of Egypt[3].

Israel had been going through much turmoil while the period of the Judges ruled, both politically and spiritually, which lasted 400 years. The book of Judges ends with this verse: *"In those days Israel had no king; everyone did as they saw fit" (ESV, Judges 21:25).* The people of Israel had been entangled in a "vortex of blood and chaos."[3] They had been enslaved and oppressed in Egypt for 400 years, and after they cried out, God sent His servant Moses to deliver them:

> *"And now the cry of the Israelites has reached me, and I have seen the way the Egyptians are oppressing them. So now, go. I am sending you to Pharaoh to bring my people the Israelites out of Egypt" (ESV, Exodus 3:9-10).*

God performed many miracles along the way, including opening the Red Sea for them to walk in dry land and closing it on the Egyptian Army, granting them victory over their oppressors (Exodus 14). God supernaturally provided food, clothing, and protection (Exodus 16) and brought them safely to the Promised Land (Joshua 3). He established them as His Holy nation in Mount Sinai and gave them the Law to guide their lives. God was faithful to His people, but they were not always faithful to God. They rebelled many times and suffered the consequences of it. Only after they cried out and repented would God forgive them and restore them:

"The LORD, the compassionate and gracious God, slow to anger, abounding in love and faithfulness, maintaining love to thousands, and forgiving wickedness, rebellion and sin. Yet he does not leave the guilty unpunished; he punishes the children and their children for the sin of the parents to the third and fourth generation" (ESV, Exodus 34:6-7).

The Israelites continued this pattern of rebellion and repentance throughout the wilderness and even after they inherited the Promised Land (Judges 2:10-15). Every time they disobeyed, they would end up oppressed by their enemies, and in a Desperate Moment, in which they decided to cry out to God for mercy (Joshua 2:16-23). While they were in the midst of trouble, they would remember the Lord, cry out to him, and repent, and the Lord would rescue them, only to go back to their own ways after that:

"The time of the judges was a miserable period in Israel's history when a vicious cycle kept repeating itself: the people fell into idolatry, God let their enemies oppress them, they cried out for deliverance, God raised up a judge to rescue them, and they fell into idolatry again. Thus, the famine mentioned here was likely a result of God judging Israel's idolatry."[4]

God had promised them blessings and protection as long as they remained obedient to him, but it was ultimately their choice to make:

"If you fully obey the LORD your God and carefully follow all his commands I give you today, the LORD your God will set you high above all the nations on earth" (ESV, Deuteronomy 28:1).

If they disobeyed, He warned them of terrible consequences they would encounter (Deuteronomy 28:15-68). The list of curses for disobedience was extensive and severe. God did not want them to experience those atrocities, so He abundantly clarified it. These consequences would only come to them if they disobeyed the covenant they had agreed to:

"This day, I call the heavens and the earth as witnesses against you that I have set before you life and death, blessings and curses. Now choose life, so that you and your children may live and that you may love the Lord your God, listen to his voice, and hold fast to him. For the Lord is your life, and he will give you many years in the land he swore to give to your fathers, Abraham, Isaac and Jacob" (ESV, Deuteronomy 30:19-20).

They knew this, but unfortunately, they would continually fall back into the same patterns of sin, oppression by their enemies, repentance, and deliverance, which occurred six times in the book of Judges alone. The book of 1 Samuel comes right after this period of 400 years, and it was considered the peak of Israel's "unfaithfulness and disloyalty to the ways of Yahweh."[5] They had "abandoned God's ways and fallen into idolatry, horrific social conditions, and a disastrous civil war."[6]

Life Lesson #1:
Learning from the Past

We do not live in ancient Israel and are not bound by the same Old Testament covenant they did. However, their human tendencies and patterns of behavior mirror ours, and there is a lot we can learn from them. Hebrews 13:7 (ESV) states, *"Remember your leaders, those who spoke to you the word of God. Consider the outcome of their way of life, and imitate their faith."* The Bible calls us to "imitate their faith," which is the area we are called to perfect. Not their traditions, rituals, or even how they dressed or did life. We are not following the Old Testament covenant and are no longer bound by their regulations. We are called to emulate the way in which they walked out their raw faith in God.

We also need to learn their stories so that we can avoid the mistakes they made: 1 Corinthians 10:6 (ESV) says, *"Now these things took place as examples for us, that we might not desire evil as they did."* The Israelites (God's chosen people) went through constant cycles of sin, desperation, repentance, and a miraculous rescue from God that saved them from their enemies. They would forget the lessons they learned (sometimes the next generation would), and the cycle would start again. The entire nation suffered the consequences of this unhealthy cycle. This is why we need to study their stories. God placed them there for a reason. We do not want to forget those lessons and fall into those unhealthy cycles.

It is important to point out that not everyone's suffering results from their own sin. We live in a fallen world, and our suffering can result from several factors. Sometimes, we suffer the consequences of wrong choices from other people. Sometimes God is simply allowing sufferings in our lives to test our faith or get us ready for greater heights. Regardless of the source of your suffering, there is hope for your situation.. Psalm 145:18-19 (ESV) states:

*"The LORD is near to all who call on him,
to all who call on him in truth.
He fulfills the desire of those who fear him;
He also hears their cry and saves them."*

God can come to the rescue right where you are. He has not forgotten about you. He hears when you call.

The Bible is filled with real-life stories that will help us navigate every issue in life. We are called to learn from them. The Holy Spirit will help us make sense of these stories and apply them to our lives. Once again, as we travel through the life of the people of faith in the Old Testament, we are not trying to emulate their religious rituals or traditions but looking at their walk of faith. They pleased God through faith and surrender to Him. Hebrews 11:1 (ESV) states: *"Now faith is the assurance of things hoped for, the conviction of things not seen. For by it the people of old received their commendation."*

As we embark on this journey through the Word of God together, I want you to be committed to hearing from the Holy Spirit and following His lead in every area of your life. I believe that if you do that, you will experience great breakthroughs and victory in your life.

Questions to Reflect

What areas of my life am I believing God for a breakthrough today?

_____

_____

_____

Am I committed to the leading of the Holy Spirit through the study of God's Word, so that I can find the truth that will set me free from that cycle?

_____

_____

_____

Breakthrough Prayer

Thank you, Lord, for providing us with the Holy Spirit as a helper in our struggles and the one who empowers us to live a life of victory. Thank You for your Word, which is still current and serves as a guide on how to live our lives. As I surrender to your lead, I pray that You will grant me victory and a breakthrough in every area of my life. Please open my eyes so I can see what You want me to see and move in the direction You want me to. In Jesus' name, I pray. Amen.

Day Two

Hannah's Hardship

Besides the political, financial, and spiritual crisis in Israel, Hannah was experiencing a crisis in her personal life. She was married to a godly and influential man named Elkanah, but Hannah could not bear children. Why was this considered a crisis?

Well, in those days in ancient Israel, a woman who could not conceive carried a lot of shame. Women's lives revolved around household duties and their children; when they could not conceive, they were excluded from most activities in life.

Women in Ancient Israel

Some of their daily duties included providing food and clothing, caring for, socializing, and educating their children, organizing the household space, performing domestic rituals, and developing social relationships with family members and neighbors.

I wonder how the women in ancient Israel managed it all. For starters, they had many more children on average than the modern household; they also had to cook from scratch, make their clothes, wash by hand, and educate their children. They employed techniques such as grinding for the grain, spinning, weaving, and sewing. They transformed wool or flax into garments or household objects.[7] They also engaged in the art of pottery painting, and they made their dishes! Last but not least, they managed their animals, stored food, and aided other women in childbirth.[8]

I could not help but wonder, so I researched and found out that children played an essential role in assisting with many of these daily responsibilities, as did other women in their families. Also, everyone lived in proximity to one another.

Another way in which they were able to cope with their many responsibilities was through their community. The community was part of their daily lives. Many activities were carried out outdoors in the courtyards when the weather was warm. They were able to prepare food, wash dishes and clothes, make pottery, baskets, and other daily-use articles, and watch the children play. The courtyard was described as "the ideal playground for children, who could be watched easily while they were helping the women of the house with chores or simply playing."[9] "The courtyard was also where women interacted with female relatives or neighbors without inhibition or restriction."[10] The kids got to play and help out, and the moms got their chores done and got to socialize while enjoying the fresh air. Talk about a win-win!

"In the cold and rainy winters, the daily activities like cooking, baking bread, and weaving took place indoors."[11] The typical house in Israel was called a 4-room house, and it was suited for extended families, as it allowed the ground floor to be subdivided as the family expanded.[12] Several generations lived in the same house so that they could all help each other, cutting the need for modern concepts like child care centers, cleaners, babysitters, and even nursing homes. This also added the value of wisdom and support in raising kids in this multi-generational environment. The kids had their grandparents to learn from, and the grandparents had the love and support they needed, as well as purpose in their old age.

Life Lesson # 2:
We Need One Another

Studies show that the United States is losing this sense of community more and more. A report titled "Our Epidemic of Loneliness and Isolation" found that "even before the COVID-19 pandemic, about half of U.S. adults reported experiencing measurable levels of loneliness."[13] It also reported that "many young people now use social media as a replacement for in-person relationships, and this often meant lower-quality connections." But we do not need to fall into these statistics. The Bible values community and calls us not to forsake it:

> *"And let us consider how we may spur one another on toward love and good deeds, not giving up meeting together, as some are in the habit of doing, but encouraging one another—and all the more as you see the Day approaching" (ESV, Hebrews 10:24-25).*

Our society is not set up like ancient Israel. Most people don't even know their neighbors; their family members live in different cities, states, or countries, and they are so busy with work and other activities that they rarely get to connect with others. But we do not have to follow the ways of our culture. God commanded us to have fellowship with one another because He made us, and He knows what we truly need. Countless passages in the Scriptures refer to life with others. It was assumed that our Christian Walk was meant to be practiced alongside other believers and not in isolation. 1 Peter 4:8-10 (ESV) states:

> *"Most important of all, continue to show deep love for each other, for love makes up for many of your faults. Cheerfully share your home with those who need a meal or a place to stay for the night. God has given each of you some special abilities; be sure to use them to help each other, passing on to others God's many kinds of blessings."*

We were not meant to live alone, "minding our own business." As inconvenient and against the grain as it might seem, we must strive to value those life skills and practices the Lord commands us to do. Life goes to the next level when we do things God's way.

Personal Story: God's Family Right on Time

I cannot say that I have this area figured out. I grew up in a Christian home, and looking back at my childhood, I see that my fondest memories were of fellowship with our church family. There was joy and love, and people were so kind to one another. I remember they were always so happy to see my sister and me. As I got older, I became busier and focused on my goals. Friendships took a backseat in my life; however, once again, as I look back, the happiest memories in every season were surrounded by my family in the faith. God always provided those people I needed for that specific season. The key has always been not to look at what the world looks at in friendships but to be open to those key people that the Lord appointed for such a time and learn to embrace and appreciate them. The way I am naturally wired, prioritizing relationships does not always come easy. The busier I get, the more isolated I tend to be, but that's when loneliness, discouragement, and other negative thoughts can easily creep in.

There was a specific time about 5 years ago when the Lord was leading my husband and me to get more involved in church. We had been busy with young children, moving, and other projects and had neglected connecting with other believers. We were very stressed out, and our priorities were not in line with God's. There is more to this story, and I will go into more detail later on. However, the point is that we obeyed His voice and got involved in several ministries and serving opportunities. It was not always easy with two young children, but we did it anyway. It wasn't long after we got connected and involved that we found out that our youngest daughter, Daniella, needed surgery. She was not even one year old at the time and had to be hospitalized for several weeks. There were some complications, and several specialists got involved. It was one of the most challenging seasons for us as parents, and most of our family lived far away. I remember holding her in my arms all night because she had little cables all over her. This is when I appreciated the body of Christ the most. They became our family. They took turns bringing us hot meals, caring for our oldest son, and visiting our daughter daily. They would come and pray for us when we needed it the most. The people we met at church during that season became our family. It would have been a very different experience if we had not listened to God and taken those small steps of obedience toward connecting with others. God made us for community, and as scary, countercultural, and inconvenient as it might seem, as we take those steps of faith, He will lead us to wonderful people who will come alongside us in our journey.

Questions to Reflect

Who do I believe God has strategically placed in my life for this specific season?

_____

_____

_____

What practical steps could I take to prioritize community, fellowship, and serving others during this time?

_____

_____

_____

Breakthrough Prayer

Thank you, Lord, for giving us your Word and showing us practical ways to live life to the fullest. Help us find those people that You want us to connect with during this season in our lives. Help us recognize those who are sent by You and those who are not a good influence in our lives and help us make wise choices. Help us understand the importance of our community of faith, and how to make it a priority. Give us those friendships that will stand the test of time and that will lead us closer to you. Show us how to use the gifts You have given us in order to serve others. Thank You that You have heard our prayers. In Jesus' name. Amen.

Day Three

Elkanah's Solution to Hannah's Problem
(1 Samuel 1:1-2)

Going back to ancient Israel, when a woman did not have children, she missed most life activities. Having many children was also a sign of social status,[14] while not having children was looked down upon. Being barren was viewed as a disgrace for a married woman in that culture, and it caused psychological distress.[15]

On the other hand, there were practical benefits to having children. Children were responsible for taking care of their parents in their old age, carrying their memories, and assisting with providing a proper burial. So, for Hannah, not having children would mean not having anyone to provide or care for her in her old age. She was part of a community, but she was socially ostracized. She had minimal options for the future.

In addition to the stigma Hannah was carrying, her husband, Elkanah, decided to take on a second wife. This was not against the law; wealthy people commonly practiced it to have children and extend their households. This practice was even more justified if their first wife could not bear children. We can see examples of this cultural practice in the story of Abraham and Sarah in Genesis 16. Childbearing was likely the main reason why Elkanah took on Peninnah. I don't have a personal frame of reference for this cultural practice, but it sounds to me like a terrible idea. However, in ancient Israel, it was "perfectly acceptable."

Life Lesson #3:
God's Ways vs. Culture

How often do we follow what is acceptable in our circles, families, countries, or societies without a second thought? Many practices commonly adopted, even among Christians, go against the Word of God, and then we wonder why things are not working out the way they should.

Even though taking on a second wife was socially acceptable, it was not God's intended plan for marriage; Genesis 2:24 (ESV) states: *"That is why a man leaves his father and mother and is united to his wife, and they become one flesh."* From the beginning of creation, God designed man to have one wife alone. He only gave Eve to Adam as his suitable helper. Then the Lord God said, "It is not good that the man should be alone; I will make him a helper fit for him" (Gen 2:18). One wife was good, and more than enough! When we deviate from God's original plan, even if a little bit, we will experience the negative consequences of those choices.

Peninnah was Elkanah's second wife, and the Bible describes her as Hannah's rival, adversary, or tormentor. She continually provoked her until Hannah wept and would not eat. Proverbs 10:22 (ESV) states, *"The blessing of the LORD makes rich, and he adds no sorrow with it."* Peninnah was not a blessing from the Lord; she was a bully. She was the result of doing things "man's way."

Peninnah constantly needed to remind Hannah that she had children and Hannah did not. This was a terrible existence for Hannah. How much worse could it get? She was not only bearing the shame of society and the sorrow of not being able to have children, but now she had to face this oppressive woman and her children as a constant reminder.

Instead of seeking a solution from God, Elkanah followed the "culture's solution" to his infertility problem. He did not adhere to God's plan for marriage, and this only brought more pain and sorrow to his family. The Bible is filled with stories of godly people like Elkanah, who followed God but not wholeheartedly. They compromised in areas that did not seem significant because they aligned with the cultural practices of that time.

When we compromise, even in seemingly small matters, the repercussions can spread rapidly across every area of our lives. The Bible states in Romans 12:2 (ESV):

"Do not conform to the pattern of this world, but be transformed by the renewing of your mind. Then you will be able to test and approve what God's will is—his good, pleasing and perfect will."

Elkanah's household was filled with tension as Peninnah became Hannah's adversary.

We as believers also have an adversary who can only access our lives when we step outside of God's perfect will, as seen in this story. 1 Peter 5:6-10 (NIV) states:

"Humble yourselves, therefore, under God's mighty hand, that he may lift you up in due time. Cast all your anxiety on him because he cares for you.

"Be alert and of sober mind. Your enemy the devil prowls around like a roaring lion looking for someone to devour. Resist him, standing firm in the faith, because you know that the family of believers throughout the world is undergoing the same kind of sufferings.

"And the God of all grace, who called you to his eternal glory in Christ, after you have suffered a little while, will himself restore you and make you strong, firm and steadfast."

The devil will come and tempt us by presenting "his plan" and "his ways" of solving our problems—this is what he did with Jesus in the desert. He will offer us "easy solutions" that can potentially destroy our lives and abort our destinies. It is precisely at this moment that we must resist him and remain firm in our faith.

It does not matter what most people in your circle would do. Even if they are good people with good intentions, their paths might look different from yours. It does not matter what your family members would like for you to do either. This is your life, and it has been uniquely designed by God with His purposes in mind.

Do not follow what seems "practical" or "easy" either. The Bible states in Isaiah 55:9 (ESV): *"For as the heavens are higher than the earth, so are my ways higher than your ways and my thoughts than your thoughts."* God's ways might not always make sense to us immediately, but if we trust Him, we will not be disappointed. Jeremiah 29:11(ESV) states:

> *"For I know the plans I have for you," declares the Lord, "plans to prosper you and not to harm you, plans to give you hope and a future."*

In the long run, God's plan will make sense and bring prosperity, protection, and purpose to our lives, just as we will discover it did in the life of Hannah.

Questions to Reflect

Are there areas of my life in which I have compromised?

_____

_____

_____

What had led me to those compromises? Is it fear of what others might say? Is it a lack of knowledge of the Word of God? Is it a lack of clarity of what God desires for me?

_____

_____

_____

What practical steps can I take to make changes so that I can please God above culture?

_____

_____

_____

Breakthrough Prayer

Lord, thank You for giving us your Word as a guide on how to live and what patterns to avoid. Just like Romans 12:2 commands us, help us not to conform to our culture's patterns but to renew our way of thinking through the study of your word so that we figure out what your perfect will is and walk in it. Bring to light any areas of compromise, even if they seem small, so that we can correct them. Forgive us if we have chosen what is easy or commonly practiced above what You command us to do and help us make the necessary changes. Thank You again for answering our prayers and for a fresh start. We love you. In Jesus' name, we pray. Amen

Day Four

Hannah's Desperate Moment (1 Samuel 1:3-8)

"Now this man used to go up year by year from his city to worship and to sacrifice to the Lord of hosts at Shiloh, where the two sons of Eli, Hophni and Phinehas, were priests of the Lord" (ESV, 1 Samuel 1:3).

Back in Ancient Israel, festivals were customary. Shiloh served as the religious capital of Israel until the Jerusalem Temple was built in the tenth century BC. Israel's holiest object, the Ark of the Covenant, resided in the Tabernacle at Shiloh until the Philistines took it and destroyed the site.[16] The feast at Shiloh was an annual event in which both men and women participated. This was the most important holiday of the year, celebrated at the end of the harvest and just before the rainy season began. It was a time when farmers could take a break from their fields for a few days and up to a week and celebrate with their families.[17]

This was Israel's leading center for worship during the Judges' era. Some believe that the "Feast at Shiloh" was, in fact, the Passover, while others think it was the "Feast of Tabernacles." Elkanah and his wives and children traveled to Shiloh yearly to offer sacrifices to the Lord. It was also customary to eat part of the meat sacrificed, and Elkanah shared part of that meat with his wives and children. However, the Bible states that: *"He gave (Hannah) a double portion, because he loved her, though the Lord had closed her womb" (ESV, 1 Samuel 1:4-5).*

Elkanah loved Hannah regardless of her ability to give him sons and daughters, and he wanted her to be happy. He would go out of his way to try to make her happy.

Unfortunately, his efforts could not satisfy Hannah, and they only made things worse, as they aggravated Peninnah. The Bible states that:

"'...her rival kept provoking her grievously in order to irritate her, pointing out the fact that she could not bear children.' This went on year after year. Whenever Hannah went up to the house of the Lord, her rival provoked her till she wept and would not eat" (ESV, 1 Samuel 1:6-7).

This was Hannah's 'Desperate Moment.' She felt powerless, a prisoner to her circumstances. She was unable to escape her barrenness because of the constant shame and humiliation of society and the relentless harassment of Peninnah. She had no hope for the future. In this particular day, after being harassed by Peninnah, Hannah "wept" and "would not eat." Picture a family celebration with many exquisite dishes and someone refusing to eat. In most cultures, this would change the mood of the entire event. Not only that, but that same person then starts weeping uncontrollably. This would be considered alarming or profusely inadequate. After all, it is a celebration! Everyone had traveled far and prepared way in advance for this event. But Hannah was not thinking about what was "properly accepted" then. The timing for her display of emotions was less than ideal, but she had had enough!

That being said, her husband, Elkanah, seemed a little bothered by her distress and instead of trying to comfort her, he decided to question her:

"Hannah, why do you weep? And why do you not eat? And why is your heart sad? Am I not more to you than ten sons?" (ESV, 1 Samuel 1:.8)

He did not seem very sympathetic; perhaps he did not know how to handle the situation. He seemed frustrated, possibly because he could not help or because she was making a scene. She was inconveniencing him and maybe even embarrassing him in front of others, how could she? But Hannah did not reply to him; she just got up and left.

Life Lesson # 4:
Do Not Seek in People What Only God Can Do for You

Elkanah might have had good intentions, but that was not enough for Hannah. He loved her, yet he could not fully comprehend the depth of her pain or find words that would be able to comfort her. Maybe He did not realize what Peninah was doing. Perhaps she was not allowed to share that with him. Regardless of the reason, it seems like Elkanah was not able to help her. Proverbs 14:10 (ESV) states: *"Each heart knows its own bitterness, and no one else can share its joy."*

The level of humiliation, cultural stigma, and hopelessness for the future that she experienced, along with the deep desire to have children, were beyond Elkanah's capacity to grasp. He tried to help her by giving her the extra portion, but that was not what she wanted. Even the love and devotion of a godly husband could not console Hannah's heavy heart.

It is a blessing to have people who love and care for us, especially if we are going through tragedy and pain. Hence, we discussed the value of community. However, we cannot rely exclusively on people. They will eventually fall short. After all, they are only human. We must always keep this in perspective, even when it comes to our spouses and other close people in our lives.

The reality is that we need God, first and foremost, to intervene on our behalf. He is the one who created us, the one who knows us the best, and the only one who can turn a bitter life into a sweet one. Psalm 139:1-15 (**NIV**) states:

> *"You have searched me, L*ORD*,*
> *and you know me.*
> *You know when I sit and when I rise;*
> *you perceive my thoughts from afar.*
> *You discern my going out and my lying down;*
> *you are familiar with all my ways.*
> *Before a word is on my tongue*
> *you, L*ORD*, know it completely.*
> *You hem me in behind and before,*
> *and you lay your hand upon me.*
> *Such knowledge is too wonderful for me,*
> *too lofty for me to attain.*
> *Where can I go from your Spirit?*
> *Where can I flee from your presence?*
> *If I go up to the heavens, you are there;*
> *if I make my bed in the depths, you are there.*
> *If I rise on the wings of the dawn,*
> *if I settle on the far side of the sea,*
> *even there your hand will guide me,*
> *your right hand will hold me fast.*
> *If I say, 'Surely the darkness will hide me*
> *and the light become night around me,'*
> *even the darkness will not be dark to you;*
> *the night will shine like the day,*
> *for darkness is as light to you.*
> *For you created my inmost being;*
> *you knit me together in my mother's womb.*
> *I praise you because I am fearfully and wonderfully made;*
> *your works are wonderful,*

I know that full well.
My frame was not hidden from you
when I was made in the secret place,
when I was woven together in the depths of the earth."

When we are desperate, our first tendency is to look around at the people in our lives for answers, comfort, and help. I have certainly been guilty of that. However, more often than not, I have been utterly disappointed. I am not suggesting that we must do life alone and never ask for help. I am saying that God should be the first one we seek for help.

2 Corinthians 1:3-4 (NIV) states:

"Praise be to the God and Father of our Lord Jesus Christ, the Father of compassion and the God of all comfort, who comforts us in all our troubles, so that we can comfort those in any trouble with the comfort we ourselves receive from God."

When I look at God for comfort first, he brings the people I need. More often than not, the person or form of help God brings will not match what we had in mind before consulting him. Why? Because He does not want us to depend on a particular person or method, but on Him alone!

> **More often than not, the person or form of help God brings will not match what we had in mind before consulting him.**

Nobody knows us as well as God does—not even our parents, spouses, or ourselves! He created us; He formed us in our mother's womb. No aspect of our lives is hidden from Him. God is the only one who can truly comfort us in our suffering and give us the help we really need.

Questions to Reflect

Do I have someone in my life that I tend to go to first during challenging times?

_____

_____

_____

How does it feel when even he/she cannot fully understand what I'm going through?

_____

_____

_____

Do I tend to go to that person or God first, when I am going through hard times?

_____

_____

_____

How would things change if I were to bring all of my concerns, burdens, and needs to God first and then reach out to them?

_____

_____

_____

Breakthrough Prayer

Dear God, thank You so much for the people in our lives: our spouses, friends, parents, children, and even our spiritual leaders. Help us be grateful for them, but never elevate them above you. Help us always to keep in perspective that they are only human and that we can only meet our deepest needs with you. Forgive us if we have set anyone or anything above you. Thank You for always being there, ready to listen to us and meet our every need. We love you. In Jesus' name, we pray. Amen.

Day Five

Hannah Took Action (1 Samuel 1:9)

After their "family meal," Hannah finally "hit rock bottom." Her situation had reached a point where she could no longer bear it. Have you ever gone to a party or social event and left more discouraged than when you arrived? It might be because some people, like Peninnah, knew how to "push your buttons" and remind you of your weaknesses or disadvantages in life. Perhaps someone with good intentions, like Elkanah, tried to help you feel better by being extra nice, but you thought they felt pity for you. This is not what you needed. Hannah's pain was so great that nothing outside of God could take it away. Her distress peaked at this family meal, and she decided to take action. The Bible states that:

> *"After they had eaten and drunk in Shiloh, Hannah rose. Now Eli, the priest was sitting on the seat beside the doorpost of the temple of the Lord" (ESV, 1 Samuel 1:9).*

Unlike Rachel, who turned to Jacob with the request, "Give me children, or else I die" (Gen 30:1), or Sarah, whose childlessness led her to hand over her slave girl, Hagar, to Abraham (Gen 16:2), Hannah turned to God.[18] This was the first and most significant decision that Hannah made: she turned to God, demonstrating her faith through her initiative and decisiveness. Hannah moved away from her desperate moment and towards her miracle.

A critical contrast arises when comparing Hannah to the priest Eli. Despite holding an official position as God's servant, Eli did not conduct the Tabernacle of God according to God's standards. The priesthood in Israel was in a complete crisis. Eli's sons, Hophni and Phinehas, served as the "priests of the Lord," but not wholeheartedly. The Scriptures tell us that "there were not many visions," and "the word of the Lord was rare" (3:1). Eli's sons were sinning against the Lord; Hophni and Phinehas had "no regard for God."[19] They disrespected the Lord by neglecting the correct procedures of the sacrifices. They would also lie to the people bringing the sacrifices, and they would consume the meat themselves. When people questioned their actions, they would threaten them. Additionally, they sinned by engaging in inappropriate relationships with the women who worked at the Tabernacle. The priesthood was characterized by corruption, immorality, and complete disrespect for God.

In contrast, Hannah's faith in God brings a freshness to the story. She was an "insignificant person," but she took a significant step of faith that later brought about the blessing and change that one would have expected from the priest. Despite being considered one of the lowest individuals in society due to her barrenness, she had the faith to believe God could hear her petition and make an impossible situation possible.

Life Lesson # 5:
Don't Look Around You

Hannah was surrounded by sin and compromise on every side. As a result, her nation, her spiritual leadership, and her relationships were in shambles. She didn't have the luxury of a great church or even her Bible to read. However, she had learned about the God of Israel and all the wonderful deeds He had done for her people through something called "oral tradition." [43] Back in those days, children were educated by their parents. They learned about the Law, the Covenant with God, and everything they had gone through as a nation through "oral narrative literature." [43] They used techniques such as "recitation, chanting, or singing," often accompanied by instruments like the harp and lyre, to pass on the history, traditions, and beliefs to the next generation. [43] In a nutshell, they memorized their history, culture, and religion through music. Hannah understood where the real answers came from—not from her wealthy and Godly husband, concerned family members, or even the priest. She didn't attempt to seek solutions from those around her; instead, she went straight to God. He was the true answer to all her problems. Hebrews 12:1-3 (ESV) states:

> *"Therefore, since we are surrounded by so great a cloud of witnesses, let us also lay aside every weight, and sin which clings so closely, and let us run with endurance the race that is set before us, looking to Jesus, the founder and perfecter of our faith, who for the joy that was set before him endured the cross, despising the shame, and is seated at the right hand of the throne of God."*

How often do we look at our church, spiritual leaders, or family members and think, "If only they were "more spiritual," "kinder," better in one area or another," then we would be closer to God? Then, we would have done the right thing. We tend to believe that if only our circumstances were perfect, we would be perfect, too. However, this does not comply with the truth of the Word of God. Adam and Eve, for example, had the perfect scenario, yet they sinned. Our shortcomings are not just the result of our imperfect surroundings,

Just like Hannah, with the help of God, we can rise up, above all the compromise and sin that surround us.

although that could be a factor. The "perfect environment" is not a guarantee for perfect results either. Although our surroundings play a role, we do have a choice. Just like Hannah, with the help of God, we can rise up, above all the compromise and sin that surround us.

Despite the difficulties, Hannah didn't give up. She did not blame others or use those challenges as an excuse for inaction. Psalm 118:6 (ESV) states: *"The Lord is on my side; I will not fear. What can man do to me?"* Hannah had many reasons to fear standing up that day, but she understood that if she did not do it her situation would never get better. She believed, and so she took action.

Questions to Reflect

What steps of faith do I feel the Lord is leading me to take?

_____

_____

_____

Am I willing to take those steps, even if I'm the only one, regardless of what others think about me?

_____

_____

_____

Breakthrough Prayer

Thank you, Lord, for being my helper. I have nothing to fear. Give me the courage to stand up to my situation in faith and move in the direction You are showing me, regardless of what others around me chose to do or say about me. Help me make the right decisions and protect me from evil as I step out in faith. You have promised never to leave me, not forsake me. I trust you. In Jesus' name, I pray. Amen.

Day Six

Hannah's Desperate Prayer (1 Samuel 1:10-12)

After Hannah got the courage to get up from the dinner table, the Bible states that:

"She was deeply distressed and prayed to the Lord and wept bitterly" (ESV, 1 Samuel 1:10).

Hannah is described in other translations as "she was in bitterness of soul." Elijah uses a similar expression in describing the Shunamite woman's deep agony after her only son's death (2 Kings 4:27). Hannah declared before the Lord "the depth of her soul's distress yearning for a child,"

"She made a vow and said, 'O Lord of hosts, if you will indeed look on the affliction of your servant and remember me and not forget your servant, but will give to your servant a son, then I will give him to the Lord all the days of his life, and no razor shall touch his head'" (ESV, 1 Samuel 1:11).

When Hannah pleaded with the Lord, saying, "Remember me and do not forget your servant," she was not merely asking to be placed in God's memory. This request implied "positive actions towards the one remembered."[19] An example of this same denotation is when God remembered Noah and stopped the rain (Gen 8:1 and Exod 2:24). A vital detail to highlight is that Hannah did not just ask for a child; she specifically requested a "male child," which aligns with Eastern tradition.[20]

Hannah's vow at the end of her prayer was "a promise to offer God something or to do something for him when He answered her prayer."[21] "A vow reveals how earnestly and intensely a person desires a favor from God."[22] "Almost all the prayers sealed with a vow in the Bible were granted by God" (Gen 28:20-22, Josh 15:16, 1 Samuel 14:24). "Whoever makes a valid vow is bound to fulfill it (see Lev 27); the only exception is an invalid vow."[23]

Hannah told God, "If only you…give to your servant a male child, then I will set him before you as a Nazarite until the day of his death." It is surprising that Hannah, who had endured childlessness all these years, vows to give back to God the child she prayed for. Hannah's vow is comparable to Abraham's willingness to offer up his only son, Isaac, as a sacrifice to the Lord (Gen 22). She voluntarily promised to offer back to God her "future" son.[24] Abraham, on the other hand, had borne Isaac after many years of childlessness and was ordered by God to give him back to him as a test of his faith (Gen 22:1). "The common denominator between Hannah and Abraham was their strong faith in God."[25] The uniqueness of Hannah's vow, apart from expressing her gratitude to God, reveals her heart's desire to bear a son (an heir) and become a mother."[26] Desperate to become a mother, she was willing to return her son to the Lord. Her prayer was bold and radical. She offered the very best she could think of to have it answered.

It is essential to clarify that it is not the "sacrifice" or "offering" that justified Abraham or that moved the hand of God for Hannah. James 2:20-24 (NIV) states the following:

> *"You foolish person, do you want evidence that faith without deeds is useless? Was not our father Abraham considered righteous for what he did when he offered his son Isaac on the altar? You see that his faith*

and his actions were working together, and his faith was made complete by what he did. And the scripture was fulfilled that says, "Abraham believed God, and it was credited to him as righteousness," and he was called God's friend. You see that a person is considered righteous by what they do and not by faith alone."

Romans 4:13 (NIV) also states that:

"It was not through the law that Abraham and his offspring received the promise that he would be heir of the world, but through the righteousness that comes by faith."

It was not a "legalistic" sacrifice that got them God's favor, but their willingness to sacrifice their only child as a demonstration of their faith in God (Gen 22:15-19). True faith is manifested in action, but it is not the action itself that is of value to God, but the faith that drove it.

Life Lesson # 6:
Spontaneous vs. Distant Prayer

Eli served as the priest and occupied the seat beside the doorpost of the temple of the Lord, which symbolized a position of high honor. Hannah did not let that intimidate her. She was unconcerned about her reputation at this point. Hannah recognized that nobody outside of God could help her. She did not approach her husband with the problem or even ask the Priest to pray for her. She believed God could hear her directly, and she went straight to Him. Her prayer was not a passive religious repetition; it emanated from her heart. The Bible states in Matthew 6:7-8 (NIV):

"And when you pray, do not keep on babbling like pagans, for they think they will be heard because of their many words. Do not be like them, for your Father knows what you need before you ask him."

Hannah was practicing spontaneous prayer. This moment was very significant because it represents "the first story of someone coming to a shrine, not for public worship or sacrifice, but simply to speak to God from the heart."[27] 1 Samuel 1:12 (ESV) states that: *"As she continued praying before the LORD, Eli observed her mouth."*

The expression "praying before" occurs here for the first time in the Old Testament. The sense is that Hannah was fully absorbed in the presence of the Lord (1 Sam 1:15: "pouring out my soul before the Lord"). She was losing herself in this prayer, not even realizing that Eli was watching.

There is a difference between the expression "praying before the Lord" and "praying to the Lord." "Praying before the Lord" emphasizes the presence of God, and "praying to the Lord" refers to the direction of the prayer; it implies a more distant type of prayer. One emphasizes a request to a distant being. Praying "before the Lord" represents an intimate relationship where the person engages their complete being—emotions, hopes, dreams, and aspirations—and surrenders them to God out of love and confidence that they are safer in His hands than in their own. Hannah's confidence that God not only cared about her deep desires but can also heal her body and turn her life around, to the point that she is willing to give it all back to Him in return, showcases true intimacy and trust. Psalm 34: 17-18 (ESV) states:

*"When the righteous cry for help, the LORD hears
and delivers them out of all their troubles.
The LORD is near to the brokenhearted
and saves the crushed in spirit."*

Even Jesus, while on earth, poured out His heart fervently to God the Father in prayer:

"In the days of his flesh, Jesus offered up prayers and supplications, with loud cries and tears, to him who was able to save him from death, and he was heard because of his reverence" (ESV, Hebrews 5:7).

When He taught the disciples how to pray and gave them what is commonly known as "The Lord's Prayer," He was giving them an example or model, but not a formula to be repeated aimlessly. As we come to terms with the fact that God is not a distant being, but He lives inside of us, and wants to have a close relationship with us, we will move away from formal, traditional, distant prayer, and into genuine, intimate, spontaneous prayer.

Questions to Reflect

If I could ask God for anything, knowing that I will get it, what would that be?

What are the top 5 things I want God to do for me?

Do I really believe He will give them to me?

If so, Am I willing to take steps of faith toward those miracles? What would some of those steps of faith look like?

Breakthrough Prayer

Lord, help me open up my heart to You without reservations and cry out from the depths of my soul, knowing that You are right here, ready to answer. Take my burdens and help me to share with You my true and honest thoughts, emotions, and desires so that You can come near and work on my behalf. Show me practical steps of faith I can take towards those things I'm believing You for, and give me the courage to do it in faith. In Jesus' name, I pray. Amen

Day Seven

Hannah's Servant's Heart

Hannah referred to herself as God's servant three times in her prayer. This is a sign of humility, surrender, and a willingness to do what the Lord asks of her. She was not demanding her way; instead, she made a deal with God. She offered the very thing she desperately sought before even receiving it. This demonstrated complete surrender. It was the best offering she could give, and she had the faith to believe for it, offering it back to the Lord in return.

Hannah's vow with the Lord was defined as the "Nazirite vow." The purpose of this vow was for someone to "separate himself for the Lord" (Numbers 6:2). This vow had several requirements, and it was usually for a limited period. Hannah's vow went even further than the traditional "Nazirite vow" (Numbers 6:21). She extended her offer to "all the days of his life." She was desperate and willing to give the Lord more than was expected or commonly acceptable as an offering. She was not trying to get away with the "minimum" offering or requirement of the law. She was giving the Lord an extravagant offering. That day, she laid everything down at the altar—her reputation, heart, and future child.

Life Lesson # 7:
More Than What's Required

Hannah's total surrender to God can be compared to Mary's offering when she poured the expensive perfume onto Jesus' feet (John 12:2-4). The disciples could not grasp the validity of this gift. To the natural eye, this was a complete waste. According to them, this perfume was worth a year's salary and could have been "sold and given to the poor." But according to Jesus, this was the right thing to do, given who He is. He is worth everything. No offering is too big, extravagant, or "irrational" when it comes to God. Hannah's intimate relationship with God meant that, just like Mary, she did not care what others thought of her or whether her reputation was on the line. She was so abandoned in His presence that nothing else mattered.

Hannah prayed "before the Lord," not "to the Lord." She was aware of God's presence in that Tabernacle and felt safe in His arms. She had no fears stopping her from offering everything without holding back. After all, the God of Heaven was the only one who held the keys to her future and could satisfy the true longings of her heart. She grasped this concept very well.

I wonder what it took for a woman back in her time to say, 'Enough is enough; I will risk it all. Nothing else matters.' She braved her fears and took action. She believed; she threw herself into the arms of a loving, all-powerful God. She "sowed" her most profound dreams and desires unto God and reaped a large harvest reaching us today.

In Philippians 4:17-19, the apostle Paul encouraged the church in Phillipi, which had sent him gifts, and called them "a fragrant offering, a sacrifice acceptable and pleasing to God." Romans 12:1 talks about offering our bodies as a "living sacrifice. Holy and acceptable to God." Hebrews 13:15-16 (ESV) specifies praise, doing good and sharing with others as sacrifices pleasing to God:

> *"Through him then let us continually offer up a sacrifice of praise to God, that is, the fruit of lips that acknowledge his name. Do not neglect to do good and to share what you have, for such sacrifices are pleasing to God."*

Even though we are not required to offer sacrifices for the forgiveness of our sins anymore (Hebrews 10), there are ways in which our giving, our actions and our worship become "Spiritual worship." Luke 6:38 (ESV) states:

> *"…give, and it will be given to you. Good measure, pressed down, shaken together, running over, will be put into your lap. For with the measure you use it will be measured back to you."*

2 Corinthians 9:6-7 (NIV) states:

> *"Remember this: Whoever sows sparingly will also reap sparingly, and whoever sows generously will also reap generously. Each of you should give what you have decided in your heart to give, not reluctantly or under compulsion, for God loves a cheerful giver."*

We get to decide how much of ourselves, our praise, our time, our talents, and our possessions we offer back to God. The more extravagant our giving, the more extravagant our return. Once we truly surrender our lives, dreams, and even our deepest sorrows to Him, we are then giving God access to begin a unique work in our hearts and lives that goes beyond anything we could have ever achieved for ourselves.

Questions to Reflect

Have I surrendered everything to the Lord as a living sacrifice yet?

_____

_____

_____

Is there any area in my life I have not fully surrendered to God yet?

_____

_____

_____

What areas have been harder to let go of: finances, relationships, career, my body, my time, my hobbies?

_____

_____

_____

Breakthrough Prayer

Lord, help me to be extravagant in my giving to You and not hold back. I offer You who I am, what I'm all about, and my hopes, dreams, and plans. I give You my talents, my weaknesses, and my strengths. I offer You my possessions, my relationships, and my time. My praise is yours. My life is yours. I will go where You want me to go. I will do what You want me to do. I will say what You want me to say. Lead me, and I will follow. My life is yours and no longer mine. In Jesus' name. Amen

Day Eight

The Priest Misinterpreted Hannah
(1 Samuel 1:13-16)

Hannah's prayer was silent. She moved her lips, wept, and poured out her heart, but nobody could hear her words to the Lord. This is the only occasion in the Old Testament in which the prayer is specified as being silent. She was not seeking pity from people; this was between her and God. Verses 13b and 14 continue, saying:

> *"Hannah was speaking in her heart; only her lips moved, and her voice was not heard. Therefore, Eli took her to be a drunken woman. And Eli said to her, 'How long will you go on being drunk? Put your wine away from you'" (ESV, 1 Samuel 1:13-14).*

"Prayer in the ancient world was almost always audible," so Eli completely misinterpreted her actions. Traditionally, prayers consisted of the person paying a fee to the priest, who, in turn, would offer a sacrifice and recite "an appropriate prayer." Hannah then replied by explaining exactly what she was doing:

> *"But Hannah answered, 'No, my lord, I am a woman troubled in spirit. I have drunk neither wine nor strong drink, but I have been pouring out my soul before the Lord'" (ESV, 1 Samuel 1:15).*

Hannah described herself as "a woman troubled in spirit" or "struggling in spirit." This expression captures Hannah's determination to take up the matter with God. Hannah responded that she had been "pouring her heart to the Lord." This is similar to the expression "praying earnestly." It denotes the "involvement of her whole being." This prayer completely consumed her.

Life Lesson # 8:
Surrendering our Reputation

The Bible urges us to do that. In Psalm 55:22 (NIV) it says:

> *"Cast your cares on the Lord*
> *and he will sustain you;*
> *he will never let*
> *the righteous be shaken."*

In Luke 22:44 (ESV), Jesus is described as "praying earnestly" before His crucifixion:

> *"And being in agony he prayed more earnestly; and his sweat became like great drops of blood falling down to the ground."*

Hannah was doing just that. She was pouring out all of her pain and suffering onto the Lord. She answered to the priest and said: *"Do not regard your servant as a worthless woman, for all along I have been speaking out of my great anxiety and vexation" (ESV, 1 Samuel 1:16).*

The expression "worthless woman" has also been translated as "wicked woman" or "base woman." It entails "without worth" or "utterly destructive woman."[28] Hannah was being misjudged and mistakenly associated with the opposite type of person she was. Still, she chose to detach herself from the opinions of others. She declared herself deeply troubled and did not want Eli to mistake her for a wicked woman.[29] After all, society had already judged her for being barren.

People will misjudge us when we choose to follow God with all of our hearts. Our motives and even our sanity might be questioned. People don't like those who are 'all in'. It exposes their hidden compromise. They might call you 'extreme,' 'radical,; or 'religious.' But do not let that deter you from giving it all to the Lord. It's so worth it!

Jesus was even misjudged. When He was delivering people from demons; the 'religious people' of the time told the crowd, "This fellow does not cast out demons except by Beelzebub, the ruler of the demons" (Matthew 12:22-29). He was also accused of being the exact opposite of who He really was. In the same way today, the enemy tries to falsely accuse God's children with lies that are the complete opposite of who they are.

Jesus was also misjudged by the priests, who handed him over to be sentenced to death: *"When morning came, all the chief priests and elders of the people plotted against Jesus to put Him to death…" (ESV, Matthew 27:1).*

The soldiers also mocked him on the way to be crucified (Matthew 27:27-32). Jesus said in Matthew 5:10-12 (NIV):

> *"Blessed are those who are persecuted because of righteousness, for theirs is the kingdom of heaven.*
> *"Blessed are you when people insult you, persecute you and falsely say all kinds of evil against you because of me. Rejoice and be glad, because great is your reward in heaven, for in the same way they persecuted the prophets who were before you."*

Paul states in 2 Timothy 3:12 (ESV) *"Yes, and all who desire to live godly in Christ Jesus will suffer persecution."* And in Matthew 5:24 (ESV), Jesus said:

"But I say to you, love your enemies, bless those who curse you, do good to those who hate you, and pray for those who spitefully use you and persecute you."

And later on:

"Behold, I send you out as sheep in the midst of wolves. Therefore be wise as serpents and harmless[] as doves. But beware of men, for they will deliver you up to councils and scourge you in their synagogues" (ESV, Matthew 10:16-17).

Just like Hannah was misjudged, even by a "Priest," when we decide to genuinely and wholeheartedly follow God, we should not be surprised when we are misinterpreted, wrongly accused, or have our motives questioned. That's part of the price to pay. Just keep moving forward, knowing that God is on your side and do not let those lies affect you one bit!

Personal Story: Persisting Amidst Opposition

I have encountered this type of persecution countless times in my life. When I was younger, God called my twin sister and me to an unusual assignment. He made it abundantly clear that He wanted us to pursue a tennis career. That was not conventional as a "calling," and I could tell people did not believe we had in fact heard from God.

At one point when we were 16 years old, we took 4 days to fast and pray and the Lord made His ultimate goal clear to us. Both of my parents found in the Sunday Newspaper an ad that said that U.S. Universities offered scholarships to Athletes from other countries. He was leading us to play tennis, so that we could get a scholarship and play for a U.S. University once we finished high school! Now our vision was clear, and we knew exactly what we were preparing for!

We continued practicing every day. We started with 2 hours a day after school at 12 years old, then we increased it to 4 hours a day during the school year and anywhere from 8 to 12 hours a day, 6 days a week during the summer break. We planned our own conditioning (led by the Holy Spirit) and followed all kinds of drills and techniques we would read on Tennis Magazines.

The Lord would open doors for us with different coaches and opportunities to improve our game, but the results were not there yet. We were not winning tournaments and our tennis career did not look promising at all. We had many people question our passion for this sport. They could not see that this was more than a sport to us, it was an assignment. We were not doing this on our own, but with God's help.

We made many sacrifices, including not attending parties, following a healthy diet, waking up at 5:30 am to exercise before school and spending almost every free moment of our day either playing tennis, reading about it, planning diets, conditioning or setting goals and working towards this dream. We would constantly pray for direction and confirmation that we were following His plan for us and not our own, and God would give us new techniques or ways of training as we did.

Coaches, peers, church leaders, and family members did not really see much of a future in us. Our dream seemed impossible, especially because we weren't "that good." It was tough at times. We did not know exactly how it would all happen. The odds were against us. But with God's help we kept persevering.

One thing we did have was the assurance that God was leading our steps. We had small 'miracles' all the time: provision, guidance, and little ways in which the Lord encouraged us to keep going and not give up. I remember at one point reading the story of Nehemiah and learning that the enemy will attempt to stop God's work by sending distractions, false accusations and discouragement. That's when we need to make a decision to follow through no matter what, and not let those things take us out. My pastor (Dan Plourde) preached recently on this same passage and He shared a verse that he quotes when those attempts of the enemy come his way: *"I am doing a great work and I cannot come down."* (Nehemiah 6:3)

When people attempt to discourage you from an assignment, they are being used by the enemy to get you off track. You should not pay attention, on the contrary, it should motivate you to move forward even more. We need to be faithful to God and take His assignments seriously, by finishing what He called us to do. This is God's assignment and not our own.

Several years later, after a lot of hard work and persistence and not seeing much evidence at all, the Lord was faithful and everything came together beautifully. We were both awarded Full Athletic Scholarships to play for one of the largest Christian Universities in the World (Liberty University)! As amazing as that was, it was just the beginning of our journey of faith. God had called us to play tennis for multiple purposes. It served as a way to get us to move to the United States, yes, but also to help us grow our faith, dependance and relationship with Him during that process.

He is faithful and His plans for each one of us are unique. We need to be able to follow His voice, even when it seems illogical or improbable. His plans for us are beautiful. Let's persevere in our obedience to God, by following His voice, and not giving up amidst opposition, taking one step of faith at a time.

Galatians 6:9 (ESV) states:

"And let us not grow weary of doing good, for in due season we will reap, if we do not give up."

If we are being mistreated, misinterpreted, or persecuted in any way for the sake of Christ, we should count it as a blessing and a confirmation that we are, in fact, His true disciples.

God said to His people, through the prophet Isaiah:

> *"Hear me, you who know what is right,*
> *you people who have taken my instruction to heart:*
> *Do not fear the reproach of mere mortals*
> *or be terrified by their insults.*
> *For the moth will eat them up like a garment;*
> *the worm will devour them like wool.*
> *But my righteousness will last forever,*
> *my salvation through all generations"* (ESV, Isaiah 51:7-8).

When we look at life through the lens of eternity, what others think of us or say about us do not seem to aggravate us as much. We are on this earth, but we are not of this earth. We have been called to fulfill a Divine assignment. Let's not allow anything or anyone to discourage us from what God is leading us to do. It's going to be worth it in the end!

Questions to Reflect

Have I ever been "persecuted" (misjudged, left out, mistreated, lied about) for following God's assignment in my life?

_____

_____

_____

Am I willing to face those repercussions for doing what God leads me to do from now on?

_____

_____

_____

Breakthrough Prayer

Thank you, Lord, for blessing me when I am willing to be persecuted or misjudged for your sake. Show me any areas in which I may have compromised out of fear of what others say about me or do. Grant me the boldness to follow your path no matter the cost. I surrender my reputation to you. I only want to please you. In Jesus' name. Amen.

Day Nine

Hannah received a Word from God
(1 Samuel 1:17-19)

Once Hannah explained her situation to the Priest, he gave her a word from the Lord, assuring her that her prayer would be answered:

> "Then Eli answered, 'Go in peace, and the God of Israel grant your petition that you have made to him.' And she said, 'Let your servant find favor in your eyes.' Then the woman went her way and ate, and her face was no longer sad" (ESV, 1 Samuel 1:17-18).

When Hannah heard that word from the priest, she knew God had heard her prayer. She had received her breakthrough right then and there, even before seeing anything tangible. Hannah was "deeply encouraged by Eli's words, which she took as God's promise."[30] She did not doubt; she believed and was instantly encouraged, even before seeing her miracle manifest.

When we fully immerse ourselves in prayer and open our hearts completely to God, we eventually experience a moment of "breakthrough" when the

> When we fully immerse ourselves in prayer and open our hearts completely to God, we eventually experience a moment of "breakthrough" when the peace of God fills our hearts, and deep inside, we know that God has heard us.

peace of God fills our hearts, and deep inside, we know that God has heard us. That prayer has been answered and we have what we have asked for. At that point, the burden is lifted from our shoulders, and we can go rejoicing, knowing that the answer is on the way! 1 John 5:14-15 (ESV) states:

> *"This is the confidence we have in approaching God: that if we ask anything according to his will, he hears us. And if we know that he hears us—whatever we ask—we know that we have what we asked of him."*

Hannah believed, rejoiced and worshipped the Lord, even before she had any evidence of the answer. She knew in her spirit that she had what she had asked for. Hannah's faith did not end there. She believed the Word of God that had been spoken by the priest, and she took action:

> *"They rose early in the morning and worshiped before the L*ORD*; then they went back to their house at Ramah. And Elkanah knew Hannah, his wife, and the L*ORD *remembered her" (ESV, 1 Samuel 1:19).*

The expression "The Lord remembered" means that God "fulfilled His agreed promises"[31]. Hannah and her husband Elkanah took a step of faith to receive the promise. Once we ask God for a breakthrough in a particular area, we are expected to take steps toward that miracle in faith.

Hannah's Miracle: More Than She Asked For! (1 Samuel 1:20 and 2:21)

> *"And in due time, Hannah conceived and bore a son, and she called his name Samuel, for she said, 'I have asked for him from the Lord'" (ESV, 1 Samuel 1:20).*

The Lord was faithful to Hannah, granting her the "male child" she had earnestly requested. But the miracle did not end there. God gave Hannah more than she had asked for or even expected. A lot more! Samuel was not just a miracle child who restored Hannah's joy and status in society and demonstrated to everyone that God was still alive and able to perform miracles. He was also the answer to the crisis that the entire nation of Israel had faced for the last 400 years. Also, the Lord blessed Hannah to have more children after Samuel. *"And the Lord was gracious to Hannah; she gave birth to three sons and two daughters. Meanwhile, the boy Samuel grew up in the presence of the LORD" (ESV, 1 Samuel 2:21).*

Life Lesson # 9:
In Due Season

Several weeks may have passed from the moment of conception until she realized that she was expecting. Even when she understood that the Lord had answered her prayer, she had to wait for the entire pregnancy for the promise to manifest fully.

There is a natural process and a perfect time for God's promises to become evident. We talked about the fact that God can rescue us from any and every situation immediately and right away. However, there are times when, even though God has already answered our prayers, the manifestation of it does not happen immediately.

This "waiting period" does not imply that God has forgotten about us or enjoys making us wait. It just means that sometimes, there is a process like sowing a seed and waiting for it to grow to harvest the fruit. Galatians 6:9 (ESV) states:

> *"Let us not become weary in doing good, for at the proper time we will reap a harvest if we do not give up."*

The word "time" in this verse comes from the Greek word "Kairos," which in the Bible has been translated as "right time," "appointed time," "harvest time," "proper time," "due season," "due time," "opportune time" or "suitable time."[32] This refers to God's perfect timing. There are certain things for which we are not quite ready for. God is waiting for us to mature or be ready to receive them.

Personal Story: The Natural Waiting Period

When I was 16 years old, and received God's assignment to move to the United States for college, I was still in High School. This meant I had to wait at least 3 years (and a lot of hard work) for that promise to be fulfilled. I remember I could hardly wait, so I tried multiple times to speed up the process! At some point, my sister and I decided to apply for an exchange program that, if we were approved, would allow us to move to the US two years sooner. We would finish High school in the US. But this was not God's timing. It would not have worked!

God had heard our prayers, and He knew what we wanted. Still, we had to finish High School first, as well as complete all the natural steps of the process, like passing the SAT exam, applying to many Universities, contacting the Tennis Coaches and many, many other steps of faith and obedience, required to attain that promise. Those 7 years from the time we started to play tennis consistently until we finally moved to the United States felt longer than we wanted them to be, but they were necessary to prepare us for what was coming.

Answered prayers aren't 'magic,' nor always instantaneous. I do believe that God has the power to heal, move in supernatural ways and turn someone's life around in a moment. However, many times He works for years in someone's life behind the scenes and all we see is the 'sudden blessings' upon them. I love this famous quote by Lionel Messi when he was a teenager and signed a contract with Barcelona "…it took me 17 years and 114 days to become an overnight success." Sometimes people underestimate the time and effort that goes behind the success of certain ministries or leadership positions. God is faithful and does His part, but we are to do our part and persevere in order for His plans to come to fruition.

Having faith does not necessarily mean we are going to take a shortcut. There are instances in which God will "drop an opportunity on our laps," and all we have to do is receive it. But there are also instances in which we are required to walk the entire process by faith, and it's only at the end that we will see His hand that orchestrated everything to come together.

James 5:7-8 (ESV) speaks of waiting patiently like the farmer:

"Be patient, then, brothers and sisters, until the Lord's coming. See how the farmer waits for the land to yield its valuable crop, patiently waiting for the autumn and spring rains. You too, be patient and stand firm, because the Lord's coming is near."

The Bible speaks about patience, not giving up, and waiting numerous times. Our tendency as a modern society is to expect everything to be instant. We are not used to waiting, and when waiting for God's promises, we can easily get discouraged, thinking there might be something wrong with the process. Habakkuk 2:3 (ESV) states:

"For still the vision awaits its appointed time; it hastens to the end—it will not lie. If it seems slow, wait for it; it will surely come; it will not delay."

The Lord does not forget about us; we must not give up during the waiting season, and we need to continue doing what the Lord already assigned us to do, as we wait for what's next.

Questions to Reflect

What promises of God am I still waiting to see fulfilled in my life?

_____

_____

_____

What specific Bible verses can I use to pray and believe that those promises will come to pass?

_____

_____

_____

Breakthrough Prayer

Thank you, Lord, that your promises are true and that You will never fail me. Give me the faith to believe that I will see your promises fulfilled in my life. Help me use this "waiting period" wisely by preparing for what's to come. Help me recognize those open doors and opportunities You are placing in my path today and take advantage of them. In Jesus' name. Amen.

Day Ten

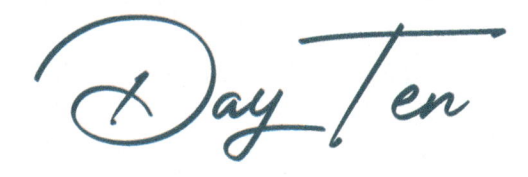

Hannah Fulfills Her Promise to God
(1 Samuel 1:21-23)

The Lord answered her prayer, and now it was Hannah's turn to fulfill the vow she had made to the Lord:

> "The man Elkanah and all his house went up to offer the Lord the yearly sacrifice and pay his vow. But Hannah did not go up, for she said to her husband, 'As soon as the child is weaned, I will bring him so that he may appear in the presence of the Lord and dwell there forever.' Elkanah, her husband, said to her, 'Do what seems best to you; wait until you have weaned him; only may the Lord establish his word.' So, the woman remained and nursed her son until she weaned him" (ESV, 1 Samuel 1:21-23).

Hannah most likely nursed the child for three years before she brought him to the priest.

She fulfilled her promise to God by bringing Samuel after he was weaned. Additionally, she sacrificed a bull and reminded Eli that this was the child she had prayed for.[33]

Hannah displayed a grateful attitude towards the Lord, going above and beyond to fulfill her vow. Despite the potential for numerous excuses, she did not falter in her commitment.

Ecclesiastes 5:4-6 (NIV) states:

> *"When you make a vow to God, do not delay to fulfill it. He has no pleasure in fools; fulfill your vow. It is better not to make a vow than to make one and not fulfill it. Do not let your mouth lead you into sin. And do not protest to the temple messenger, "My vow was a mistake." Why should God be angry at what you say and destroy the work of your hands?"*

Hannah did what she said she would do, and thus, she reflected the character of God, who always fulfills His promises to us.

Life Lesson # 10: Obedience vs. Sacrifices

There is no greater way to show God that we love him than by being obedient to His voice and submissive to him.

> *…"Does the LORD delight in burnt offerings and sacrifices as much as in obeying the LORD? To obey is better than sacrifice, and to heed is better than the fat of rams" (ESV, 1 Samuel 15:22).*

God delights in obedience and yielding to Him over empty sacrifices. However, once we live a life of obedience to God, we can take it a step further and show Him our devotion by sacrificing our time and resources for His purposes. Sacrifices with the wrong motives are detestable to the Lord; He can see the deepest parts of our hearts. On the same token, genuine love for God should eventually be accompanied by outward manifestations. Luke 6:46-49 (NIV) states:

> *"Why do you call me, 'Lord, Lord,' and do not do what I say? As for everyone who comes to me and hears my words and puts them into practice, I will show you what they are like. They are like a man*

building a house, who dug down deep and laid the foundation on rock. When a flood came, the torrent struck that house but could not shake it, because it was well built. But the one who hears my words and does not put them into practice is like a man who built a house on the ground without a foundation. The moment the torrent struck that house, it collapsed and its destruction was complete."

When guided by His Spirit, Sacrifices become a fragrant aroma to Him and the key to supernatural blessings. However, they are not the type of sacrifices of the Old Testament but rather giving either time, material possessions, or even our plans, agendas or comfort for the work of the Lord.

Personal Story: Sowing My Accomplishments

I remember this certain evening in the Summer of 2006, at a Church youth group in Boca Raton, Fl, after I had graduated with my Bachelor's degree. It was the time of the offering and I felt like the Lord wanted me to "sow" (give Him an offering) my accomplishment to Him. I had a silver ring my aunt had given me as a Graduation gift with the logo of my University on it. I remember this accomplishment had meant so much. All those years of believing and working towards that Scholarship and then all the years of competing, studying and trusting God for strength and provision at every turn. This was painful, not because of the gift's monetary value, but because it symbolized my most outstanding achievement. But I did it anyway. I remember I sowed it in the youth group offering, and the lady taking it up wanted to give it back to me. She thought it had fallen off my hand! I said, no, "I want to give that to the Lord." I felt God wanted me to give up something that symbolized an "idol" to me. That way, He would be first in my heart and could eventually bless me with even greater achievements. Surely enough, It's been

18 years since that moment and the Lord has been exceedingly good to me. Along the way, He has asked me to give up things that meant a lot to me to prove that He was still first in my heart, and as hard as it was at the time, I always knew it would be so worth it!

When the Lord places a specific offering on our hearts, He has a harvest in mind for us. He also knows that we cannot move forward if that object, career, or relationship we are 'sacrificing' holds our hearts. When God asks us to give something up for Him, He is in fact seeking to set us free from what's holding us back!

> When God asks us to give something up for Him, He is in fact seeking to set us free from what's holding us back!

Hannah gave back to God everything she had. Her son represented her dreams, hopes, job, societal reputation, retirement, hope for the future, joy, and the reason for being alive. She sacrificially offered it to the Lord, acknowledging that He was the one who initially gave it to her. In doing so, she recognized God as the giver of life and the source of everything we could ever need.

Questions to Reflect

Is there anything, material or symbolic, that I'm feeling led to sow to the Lord today?

_____

_____

_____

Breakthrough Prayer

Thank you, Lord, for your faithfulness in my life. Thank You for your provision, protection, and countless promises I can rely on for my every need. Show me if anything in my life that You require for me to sow to you. Show me anything that might be first in my heart before you. You are welcome to have it. You are my source of provision, happiness, comfort, and purpose. In Jesus' name. Amen.

Day Eleven

Hannah's Offering (1 Samuel 1:24-28)

Hannah surrendered everything to God. Her sacrifice can be compared to Abraham, who was willing to sacrifice his only son in obedience to God. This act of obedience, complete surrender, and letting go of her own dreams became the key that unlocked her destiny, revealed the purpose for her life, and paved the way for the supernatural future of her son, Samuel:

> *"And when she had weaned him, she took him up with her, along with a three-year-old bull, an ephah of flour, and a skin of wine, and she brought him to the house of the Lord at Shiloh. And the child was young" (ESV, 1 Samuel 1:24).*

Hannah not only sacrificed her one and only son by bringing him to the House of the Lord to be trained as a Priest, but she did so with a joyful and thankful heart. Additionally, she attached a generous offering to it. She felt honored to dedicate her child to the service of the Lord. Humbly recognizing that the child was a gift from the Lord in the first place, Hannah presented both a substantial animal offering and a flour offering."[34]

> *"Then they slaughtered the bull, and they brought the child to Eli. And she said, 'Oh, my lord! As you live, my lord, I am the woman who was standing here in your presence, praying to the Lord. For this child I prayed, and the Lord has granted me my petition that I made to*

him. *Therefore, I have lent him to the Lord. As long as he lives, he is lent to the Lord.' And he worshiped the Lord there"* (ESV, 1 Samuel 1:25-28).

"Joyfully, Hannah points to this boy as the answer to that prayer,"[35] and she "performs the act of dedication."[36] She gives her son back to the Lord "in a true act of worship."[37]

This was another instance where Hannah put her faith into action. She did not just express gratitude to the Lord; instead, she thanked God through worship and sacrificial giving.

Life Lesson # 11:
Heart Worship vs Lip Service

In 2 Samuel 24:24 (ESV), King David said: *"I will not sacrifice to the LORD my God burnt offerings that cost me nothing."* In our society, we have grown accustomed to receiving blessings from the Lord, but we often do not feel the need to bless the Lord back. The Bible teaches that the Lord sees our hearts. And even though this is true, it does not mean that our "good intentions" alone are sufficient for Him. In fact, our actions are reflections of our hearts.

When we love a friend or family member, merely saying "I love you" falls short; we must demonstrate our love by being present for them in times of distress and by assisting them with practical actions. That is sacrificial love. The same principle applies to our relationship with the Lord. In Matthew 25:35-40 (ESV), Jesus said:

> *"'For I was hungry and you gave me food, I was thirsty and you gave me drink, I was a stranger and you welcomed me, I was naked and you clothed me, I was sick and you visited me, I was in prison and you came to me.' Then the righteous will answer him, saying, 'Lord, when did we see you hungry and feed you, or thirsty and give you drink? And when*

did we see you a stranger and welcome you, or naked and clothe you? And when did we see you sick or in prison and visit you?' And the King will answer them, 'Truly, I say to you, as you did it to one of the least of these my brothers, you did it to me.'"

Helping other people by using our time and giftings is a way to demonstrate our love for the Lord. Financial giving to either support God's work or to help those in need is another way to manifest our love and trust towards Him. Additionally, the words we choose to speak, how we treat those around us, and the choices we make all have the potential to glorify God. Even our physical bodies can be considered offerings of worship to the Lord, as Romans 12:1 states: *"I appeal to you therefore, brothers, by the mercies of God, to present your bodies as a living sacrifice, holy and acceptable to God, which is your spiritual worship."* Our daily work, when done wholeheartedly for the Lord, is also a way to bring an offering. Colossians 3:23 (ESV) states: *"Whatever you do, work heartily, as for the Lord and not for men…"* James 2:20 (ESV) states: *"Do you want to be shown, you foolish person, that faith apart from works is useless?"* Jesus said in Matthew 7:20 (NLT): *"Yes, just as you can identify a tree by its fruit, so you can identify people by their actions."*

Personal Story: Dating

When I was single and dating, I was never interested in someone who was "casual" about me. I was not okay with someone who would text me one day and then forget about me for two weeks, only to call me again when he was bored. I did not like to play games. It felt disrespectful and a complete waste of my time. I wanted to meet someone who knew what he wanted and could recognize it in me right away. My husband is like that. He told me that as soon as he met me, he knew I would be his wife. He did not hesitate; he invited me out again right away, invited my family over for a BBQ, and ended up proposing to me a few months later.

That is exactly the nature of God. He pursues us and seeks a real commitment from us. I'm not saying that God is not patient with us. He understands where we are in our walk with Him. However, he wants us to pursue His Kingdom above everything else, and there will be a point in which we will be tested. If we are casual about him, we will reap the consequences of that attitude. Galatians 6:7-8 (ESV) states:

> *"Do not be deceived: God is not mocked, for whatever one sows, that will he also reap. For the one who sows to his own flesh will from the flesh reap corruption, but the one who sows to the Spirit will from the Spirit reap eternal life."*

We receive God's salvation by grace, through faith in Christ and His work on the cross. Yet, to fully partake in the abundant life God has prepared for us, we must genuinely surrender every aspect of our lives and follow Him wholeheartedly. Matthew 6:33 (ESV) states: *"But seek first the kingdom of God and his righteousness, and all these things will be added to you."*

Hannah, in her desperation, recognized that without God's intervention, her situation wouldn't improve; it might even worsen. Consequently, she surrendered everything to the Lord, including her only child. God, acknowledging her surrendered heart, worked miraculous wonders for her. While Samuel was the initial miracle, Hannah's surrender resulted in an extraordinary harvest extending far beyond her time. God can do the same for us if we are willing to give Him the first place in our hearts.

Questions to Reflect

Do I want to go to the next level with God?

_____

_____

_____

What sacrifices am I willing to make to get there?

_____

_____

_____

What am I willing to offer God as tangible proof that I am serious about putting His Kingdom above everything else in my life?

_____

_____

_____

Breakthrough Prayer

Show me, Lord, how to live a life that expresses true devotion to you. Please help me find tangible ways to serve you. Help me show You with actions how grateful I am for what you've done for me and how serious I am about living for you. In Jesus' name. Amen.

Day Twelve

Hannah's Grateful Heart (1 Samuel 2:1-10)

Hannah's prayer of thanksgiving, when she offered Samuel for his service reflects her heart of gratitude, her humble spirit, and a deep understanding of the nature of God:

And Hannah prayed and said,

"My heart exults in the Lord;
my horn is exalted in the Lord.
My mouth derides my enemies,
because I rejoice in your salvation.

"There is none holy like the Lord:
for there is none besides you;
there is no rock like our God.

Talk no more so very proudly,
let not arrogance come from your mouth;
for the Lord is a God of knowledge,
and by his actions are weighed.

The bows of the mighty are broken,
but the feeble bind on strength.

Those who were full have hired themselves out for bread,
but those who were hungry have ceased to hunger.
The barren has borne seven,
but she, who has many children, is forlorn.

The Lord kills and brings to life;
he brings down to Sheol and raises.
This verse refers to the 'sovereignty of God.'

The Lord makes poor and makes rich;
he brings low, and he exalts.

He raises the poor from the dust;
he lifts the needy from the ash heap
to make them sit with princes
and inherit a seat of honor.
For the pillars of the earth are the Lord's,
and on them he has set the world.

"He will guard the feet of his faithful ones,
but the wicked shall be cut off in darkness,
for not by might shall a man prevail.

The adversaries of the Lord shall be broken to pieces;
against them he will thunder in heaven.
The Lord will judge the ends of the earth;
he will give strength to his king
  and exalt the horn of his anointed" (ESV, 1 Samuel 2:1-10).

Hannah testifies that God humbles the proud and exalts the weak (2:3–9) and also points out that the Lord looks upon the humble and changes the fate of the poor, the oppressed, and the needy (2:4-8). He has the power to turn any and every situation around.

Her prayer can be comparable to the Prayer of Mary in the New Testament in Luke 1:46-55, when Mary met up with Elizabeth and received confirmation that she had heard from the Lord. Hannah's thanksgiving prayer or song is also considered prophetic, as the final verses (2:10) predict Samuel's role in establishing a Monarchy for the Israelites.

Life Lesson # 12:
Gratitude Before the Breakthrough

Hannah possessed two characteristics that are rare in today's world: a humble attitude before God and gratefulness. These are requirements for us to be blessed. Hannah could have complained that she was 'leaving her son at the Temple at such a young age,' but she thanked God instead. She could have become prideful because of the 'great sacrifice' she made for the Lord, but she did not. She gave all the praise to God, who looks at the heart and notices things others do not. In the eyes of society, and quite frankly, her own family, there was no hope for her future, but in the eyes of God, her life was just getting started. She needed God, and she humbly acknowledged that.

This was only the beginning of God's blessings for her, as we will see in the following pages. She responded in gratefulness and opened the door for many more blessings. The Bible encourages us to praise the Lord and rejoice at all times, not when we have everything we want but in all circumstances and at all times. 1 Thessalonians 5:16-18 states: *"Rejoice always, pray without ceasing, give thanks in all circumstances; for this is the will of God in Christ Jesus for you."*

Psalm 9:1-2 (ESV) states:

*"I will give thanks to the L*ORD *with my whole heart;*
I will recount all of your wonderful deeds.
I will be glad and exult in you;
I will sing praise to your name, O Most High."

Personal Story: Perspective

As I was praying about a few issues in my life, the Lord brought to mind an image of a moment in time. About 8 years prior, I was at the Walmart customer service line with my son. He was young and it took a lot of patience to stay in that long line. The Lord then reminded me that I had lived in that area several years before that when I was not even married yet. All of a sudden, I could re-live the feelings of loneliness of those evenings after work, having no one to share my life with. I then realized how far He has brought me through, only in the past 8 years! As hard as that season seemed, it was a huge answered to prayer in comparison where I used to be!

Today I am married, we have 3 children, and I can serve God through my writing. So much has changed, so many answered prayers. Sometimes, we get caught up in the prayers that have not been answered yet, and miss all the good that God has already done for us! I am living the life I once dreamed of. I am walking in the result of many answered prayers and God's faithfulness in my life. Am I acknowledging that, or am I always looking at the next season, missing the blessings already right before my eyes?

Sometimes, we get caught up in the prayers that have not been answered yet, and miss all the good that God has already done for us!

The Bible calls us to have a humble heart in order to be exalted.

James 4:10 (ESV) says: *"Humble yourselves before the Lord, and he will exalt you."*

And 1 Peter 5:6-7 (ESV) states:

"Humble yourselves, therefore, under the mighty hand of God so that at the proper time he may exalt you, casting all your anxieties on him, because he cares for you."

Isaiah 66:2b (ESV) states:

"But this is the one to whom I will look:
he who is humble and contrite in spirit
and trembles at my word."

As we show gratitude and praise for the blessings the Lord has already given us, we demonstrate a humble heart toward him and position ourselves to continue to receive from Him.

Questions to Reflect

What prayers has the Lord already answered in my life that can help me put my present situation into perspective?

_____

_____

_____

List 10 things you are grateful for:

_____

_____

_____

Breakthrough Prayer

Thank you, Lord, so much for everything You have provided for me so far. I am grateful for being alive, for salvation and for having your promises to stand on, even when life gets tough. I am grateful for how far You have brought me through and how many obstacles You have moved out of my way for me to be here today. Help me not to get discouraged when things don't look "picture perfect," and help me to see life from your perspective, with a humble heart. Please help me to be grateful for the little victories on the way to the big breakthroughs. In Jesus' name, I pray. Amen.

Day Thirteen

Hannah's Legacy

The story of Hannah, up until this point, appears to be an account of a woman in distress, who asked God for a miracle and was able to receive it. This could be a satisfying ending in itself, but it is not the end. In fact, Hannah's miracle was only the beginning.

Hannah's miracle son, Samuel, ended up being called by the Lord to play a significant role in the history of ancient Israel. Although the nation had been governed by Judges, appointed by God, it had "degenerated both morally and politically"[38] and faced the relentless onslaught of the Philistines. The temple at Shiloh had been desecrated and led by a corrupt and immoral priesthood.[39] Despite being freed from slavery in Egypt, the people of Israel had suffered for 400 years. While Hannah was desperate for a child, Israel was desperate for a righteous leader, and God answered both desperate prayers through one person, Samuel.

God provided Israel with Samuel, who "set Israel on the path towards monarchy."[40] He served as a Judge "all the days of his life." He anointed Saul as King and eventually anointed King David, who was the ancestor of the Messiah, the Lord Jesus Christ.

Upon Samuel's death, "all Israel assembled and mourned for him" (25:1). He was referenced in Jeremiah 15:1 as "a second Moses,"[41] that helped deliver the people of Israel from their misery. Samuel was "the last and greatest judge"[42] after centuries of pain and suffering in the nation of Israel. Hannah's faith and sacrifice to the Lord resulted in a legacy beyond her lifetime. This is the type of legacy God can achieve through the lives of those who humble themselves before Him and cry out for help.

God's intentions go beyond blessing us and meeting our immediate needs; He desires to make our lives count for His eternal purposes. Regardless of who we are or how impossible our situation may seem, when we truly surrender to the Lord and follow His ways, He can turn our tragedy into a legacy.

Life Lesson # 13:
God Chooses the "Least Likely to Succeed"

In the eyes of the world, Hannah seemed to have no hope, no future, and no apparent value. However, from God's perspective, Hannah's tragedy served as a setup for a remarkable faith journey that would unfold into a much greater purpose. Although she could have succumbed to despair or harbored bitterness due to her challenging circumstances, she made the courageous choice to turn to God.

Against all odds, Hannah's life underwent a transformative journey. She transitioned from a state of barrenness to fruitfulness, from weeping to rejoicing, and from a posture of begging to offering her greatest blessing to God. Instead of yielding to hopelessness, she chose faith, and in doing so, her narrative was rewritten into a story of resilience, triumph, and a deep connection with God.

God, in return, did not just answer her prayer for a son. He also graciously gave her three more sons and two daughters (1 Samuel 2:21), totaling 6 children! He is the God of "more than enough." 2 Corinthians 9:8 (ESV) states:

And God is able to bless you abundantly, so that in all things at all times, having all that you need, you will abound in every good work.

Ephesians 3:20-21(ESV) states:

"Now to him who is able to do immeasurably more than all we ask or imagine, according to the power that is at work within us, to him be glory in the church and in Christ Jesus throughout all generations, forever and ever! Amen."

There is nothing too hard for the Lord; there are no circumstances He cannot reverse, and there is no life He cannot turn around. He makes a way where there seems to be no way. There is a well-known Psalm that states this beautifully:

Psalm 146 states:

"Praise the LORD.
Praise the LORD, my soul.
I will praise the LORD all my life;
I will sing praise to my God as long as I live.
Do not put your trust in princes,
in human beings, who cannot save.
When their spirit departs, they return to the ground;
on that very day their plans come to nothing.
Blessed are those whose help is the God of Jacob,
whose hope is in the LORD their God.
He is the Maker of heaven and earth,
the sea, and everything in them—
he remains faithful forever.
He upholds the cause of the oppressed
and gives food to the hungry.
The LORD sets prisoners free,
the LORD gives sight to the blind,
the LORD lifts up those who are bowed down,
the LORD loves the righteous.

*The LORD watches over the foreigner
    and sustains the fatherless and the widow,
    but he frustrates the ways of the wicked.
The LORD reigns forever,
    your God, O Zion, for all generations.
Praise the LORD" (NIV, Psalm 146:1-10).*

The prevailing cultural message of our time assumes that, to succeed, one must possess the "ideal set of circumstances." Specific attributes such as upbringing, resources, education, opportunities, and abilities are necessary to gain admission to the most prestigious universities. People tend to focus on these factors as indicators of "potential" in an individual. The prevailing notion is that one will not achieve much without a perfect background. This can be highly discouraging for the majority of people. Even those belonging to privileged societal groups feel compelled to excel at increasingly higher levels and in unique ways just so their efforts can be recognized.

This pressure extends to parents who may feel overwhelmed when attempting to provide their children with the "right" upbringing. Moreover, given these unattainable standards, it is particularly disheartening for those facing some form of "disadvantage," similar to Hannah's situation in ancient Israel.

Nevertheless, God's ways surpass ours. He elevates the lowly, the forgotten, and those deemed least likely to succeed, using them to accomplish His most remarkable work. The passage in 1 Corinthians 1:26-31 (ESV) underscores this divine perspective:

"Brothers and sisters, think of what you were when you were called. Not many of you were wise by human standards; not many were influential; not many were of noble birth. But God chose the foolish things of the world to shame the wise; God chose the weak things of the world to shame the strong. God chose the lowly things

of this world and the despised things—and the things that are not—to nullify the things that are, so that no one may boast before him. It is because of him that you are in Christ Jesus, who has become for us wisdom from God—that is, our righteousness, holiness and redemption. Therefore, as it is written: "Let the one who boasts boast in the Lord."

God does not assess individuals based on their "worldly credentials"; He does not disqualify anyone according to the standards set by our culture. His criteria are distinctly different. Every person is afforded an equal opportunity to be saved by God, used by Him, and lead a life that holds genuine significance. The parable of the widow and the two mites (Luke 21:1-4) and the parable of the talents (Matthew 25:14-30) are two examples of this principle, where it is not about what we accomplish in comparison with others, but concerning what we had to begin with. God gives us all a fair chance, which does not mean an equal chance. Everyone has a different playing field with a different set of circumstances. We all have unique races to run.

> **Every person is afforded an equal opportunity to be saved by God, used by Him, and lead a life that holds genuine significance.**

Psalm 51:16-17 (ESV) expresses this perspective:

"You do not delight in sacrifice, or I would bring it;
you do not take pleasure in burnt offerings.
My sacrifice, O God, is a broken spirit;
a broken and contrite heart
you, God, will not despise."

Proverbs 3:34 (ESV) states:

*"He mocks proud mockers
but shows favor to the humble and oppressed."*

James 4:6-10 (ESV) states:

"But he gives us more grace. That is why Scripture says:

*'God opposes the proud
but shows favor to the humble.'
Submit yourselves, then, to God. Resist the devil, and he will flee from you. Come near to God and he will come near to you. Wash your hands, you sinners, and purify your hearts, you double-minded. Grieve, mourn, and wail. Change your laughter to mourning and your joy to gloom. Humble yourselves before the Lord, and he will lift you up."*

God is looking for people who, like Hannah, are desperate for Him. People willing to obey His voice surrender their whole being to Him without reservations. God is not a "genie" to whom we pray and ask him for what we want. He is not a vending machine, either. God is our creator. He is merciful to the humble but rejects the proud and arrogant. He cannot use the people that boast of their abilities.

So, if you are going through a Desperate Situation, do not get discouraged. The Lord can turn your situation around and use your life meaningfully above your wildest dreams. Your hardship or "disadvantage" in life today might be the one thing God uses to take you where you need to go. 2 Corinthians 12:9-11 (ESV) states:

"But he said to me, 'My grace is sufficient for you, for my power is made perfect in weakness.' Therefore, I will boast all the more gladly about my weaknesses, so that Christ's power may rest on me. That is why, for Christ's sake, I delight in weaknesses, in insults, in hardships, in persecutions, in difficulties. For when I am weak, then I am strong."

Psalm 34:18 (ESV) states:

*"The LORD is close to the brokenhearted
and saves those who are crushed in spirit."*

God is ready to answer your prayer.
Psalm 116:1(ESV) states:

*"I love the Lord, for he heard my voice;
he heard my cry for mercy."*

Jeremiah 33:2-3 (ESV) states:

"This is what the Lord says, he who made the earth, the Lord who formed it and established it—the Lord is his name: 'Call to me and I will answer you and tell you great and unsearchable things you do not know.'"

Psalm 145:18-19 (ESV) states:

*"The Lord is near to all who call on him,
to all who call on him in truth.
He fulfills the desires of those who fear him;
he hears their cry and saves them."*

The Bible is filled with verses about someone "calling out to the Lord" during a hard situation. He responds and can turn the hardest, seemingly impossible circumstances around. It's never too late to call on Him. In Luke 23: 39-43 (ESV) Jesus was able to save one of the criminals as he was hanging from the cross next to him:

"One of the criminals who hung there hurled insults at him: 'Aren't you the Messiah? Save yourself and us!'

"But the other criminal rebuked him. 'Don't you fear God,' he said, 'since you are under the same sentence? We are punished justly, for we are getting what our deeds deserve. But this man has done nothing wrong.'

Then he said, 'Jesus, remember me when you come into your kingdom.'

Jesus answered him, 'Truly I tell you, today you will be with me in paradise.'

All you have to do is believe and ask in faith. Pour out your heart to Him. Surrender your whole being—your pain, your joys, your past, present, and future to Him, and be willing to listen to His direction. Tell Him what you really want in your own words. Be real; He already knows what you are thinking. The key to answered prayer is faith, surrender, and a willingness to do what He directs you.

Hannah's life had a happy ending but did not start that way. She had to trust that God could help her, risk her reputation, get out of her situation, and take action towards her miracle. She had to place her complete hope in God and not in people. Will you trust Him that way today?

Questions to Reflect

Do I believe God can turn my life around and use me to fulfill His purposes on earth?

_____

_____

_____

What limitations or weaknesses do I carry that I need God to intervene and turn into a Testimony?

_____

_____

_____

Breakthrough Prayer

Thank you, Lord, for your Word. Thank you. My life is not a mistake, and my circumstances are not too far gone or too difficult for you. I surrender those "disadvantages" or "weaknesses", as well as the limitations, whether it is upbringing, education, emotional baggage, finances, or anything else that looks like it's keeping me from accomplishing your purpose for me. Take those seemingly impossibilities and make a way where there seems to be no way. Open up doors for me that no man can shut and use my life meaningfully for Your glory. Take the good and the bad, the pretty and the ugly, and make my life into a masterpiece that showcases Your power, love, and mercy for this broken world. I am willing to trust You and follow You every day of my life, no matter what comes my way. In Jesus' name. Amen.

Day Fourteen

Main Takeaways from Hannah's Life

Thank you for coming alongside me on this long journey through Hannah's life. My heart is that you were blessed and that the Lord was able to speak to you through the many lessons that can be found in the details, which we would most likely miss when we skim through it.

In summary, we could see how the Bible was written for our instruction. Even though some of these stories happened thousands of years ago, many miles away in a very different context, when we break them down, we can realize how they were people just like you and me and how their dilemmas and problems were not so distant from the ones we face today. We learned about the value of relationships and making the necessary sacrifices to connect with other believers, even when it's considered inconvenient in our culture today. We also learned that culture might want to dictate "common sense" solutions to our problems, but if these solutions do not align with God's plan for us, they will lead to even more significant difficulties.

One of the most powerful lessons from her life was that she chose to go to God with her problems instead of man. God was the source of her hope and did not disappoint her. We also learned not to compare our lives with other people's, even if they are believers, because we are all uniquely crafted and called, and not to concern ourselves with what others are doing around us. The "perfect environment" is not necessarily conducive to perfect results.

We also discussed the difference between spontaneous and distant prayer and going the extra mile when serving and offering something to God. To succeed in life, we also need to be able to surrender our reputation and what others might think or say about us. We also need to learn that faith without action is dead. After we pray, we need to follow up with real action. Our actions prove to God that we believe that He is working on our behalf, as opposed to inaction, which is usually based on fear and doubt.

In the last section of her story, we learned that sometimes the answer to our prayers is on the way, and we are in a season of waiting for it to manifest. We learned the difference between obedience and sacrifice and how they should go hand in hand. We learned about true worship and the importance of practicing gratefulness to position our lives to receive our breakthrough.

The last lesson encompasses the heart of this story and the fact that God delights in choosing the "underdogs" and raising them for His glory. He tends to choose the "least likely to succeed." The Lord made this principle clear in the same book of the Bible just a few chapters later:

> "But the LORD said to Samuel, 'Do not look on his appearance or on the height of his stature, because I have rejected him. For the LORD sees not as man sees: man looks on the outward appearance, but the LORD looks on the heart'" (ESV, 1 Samuel 16:7).

We often focus on the actual circumstances and our natural ability or inability to turn them around. Still, the Lord is able and willing and delights in making the impossible happen. He only requires us to hand over our lives to Him and trust Him with everything that concerns us. He loves to make heroes out of ordinary people. He loves to take the most challenging circumstance and turn it into a beautiful masterpiece. He is more than able. Do you believe that can be your story too?

Questions to Reflect

What areas of breakthrough have I already experienced during the past 14 days?

_____

_____

_____

What else would I like to see the Lord do for me, my family, or others by the end of this 40-day journey?

_____

_____

_____

My Prayer Over You

Thank you, Lord, for my brothers and sisters who have started this journey alongside me. I pray that God gives you breakthrough, victory, protection, and wisdom, making a way where there seems to be no way. I also pray that He replaces that desperation with a deep desire to live for Him, please Him, and get to know Him better daily. May you sense His presence and fall in love with Him and His word like never before. I pray for His truth to light up your path, bringing hope, joy, and freedom in every area of your life. May He take your burdens, fears, worries, and struggles, lightening your burden.

I also pray for understanding as you read the Scriptures and clarity of purpose for your life as you seek His will. May you be able to surrender to God in every area without fear, knowing that He will never leave you nor forsake you (Hebrews 13:5) and that He who began the good work in you will carry it on to completion (Philippians 1:6). May He heal your broken heart and fill you with great expectation for the future, His joy, and His peace (Isaiah 61:1). In Jesus' name, I pray. Amen.

Chapter 2:

Jonah: From Fugitive to Faithful

Days 15-26

Day Fifteen

Background on Jonah and the Nation of Israel

This Book of the Bible is often regarded as a "Prophetic Biography." It narrates the story of Jonah, an Israelite prophet from Gath-Hepher, in the northern Kingdom of Israel. To provide context, his life unfolded roughly 400 years after the time of Samuel, as depicted in the story of Hannah, spanning from 782 to 753 B.C., during the reign of King Jeroboam II. Jonah is known to have prophesied military triumph to Jeroboam II, as recorded in 2 Kings 14:25 (ESV):

> "He restored the border of Israel from Lebo-hamath as far as the Sea of the Arabah, according to the word of the Lord, the God of Israel, which he spoke by his servant Jonah, the son of Amittai, the prophet, who was from Gath-Hepher."

During Jonah's prophetic tenure, Israel experienced financial prosperity but was spiritually bankrupt. King Jeroboam II, though considered wicked in the eyes of the Lord, witnessed the territorial expansion of Israel reminiscent of King Solomon's era. Regrettably, amid this period of affluence, Israel's society became increasingly materialistic. Their actions were marked by injustice towards the marginalized and oppressed, a phenomenon foretold by Amos, a contemporary prophet of Jonah. The Nation of Israel allowed material prosperity to distract them from God. Their financial success blinded them, and they began acting in direct contradiction with God's standards.

Life Lesson # 15:
Remain Humble in Prosperity

One of the characteristics of the Nation of Israel, throughout the Old Testament, was the vicious cycle of disobedience, repentance, change of heart, blessings of God, and right back to disobedience. They had difficulty keeping their priorities aligned with God's when the blessings started pouring in.

Nowadays, we run the very same risk. See, God wants to prosper us in every area of our lives. In health, finances, spirituality, emotions, and relationships. 3 John 2:2 states:

> *"Beloved, I pray that you may prosper in every way and [that your body] may keep well, even as [I know] your soul keeps well and prospers" (AMPC).*

It is not wrong to be blessed, prosperous, or abundant. It is God's will for all His children to enjoy blessings and increase. The Godliest Old Testament heroes were extremely wealthy (Abraham, Isaac, Solomon, David, Joseph), and the list goes on. In Genesis 26:12-13 (ESV) we see just one of the many examples of this truth:

> *"And Isaac sowed in that land and reaped in the same year a hundredfold. The LORD blessed him, and the man became rich, and gained more and more until he became very wealthy."*

God is the same yesterday, today, and forever. He doesn't change, and if He led His people to prosperity then, He also wants to do it for us today. The key in these situations is that His

> **God is the same yesterday, today, and forever. He doesn't change, and if He led His people to prosperity then, He also wants to do it for us today.**

children keep Him first when He prospers them. Matthew 16:26 (ESV) states:

> *"For what will it profit a man if he gains the whole world and forfeits his soul? Or what shall a man give in return for his soul?"*

God wants us to be blessed, but not at the cost of our souls, and for that to be avoided, we must keep God at the throne of our hearts. Money and possessions were never an issue when kept in perspective. The more they followed the Lord, the more He led them to conquer new territories and obtain material possessions. These promises to Abraham and his offspring now apply to us by faith. Galatians 3:13-14 (ESV) states:

> *"Christ redeemed us from the curse of the law by becoming a curse for us—for it is written, "Cursed is everyone who is hanged on a tree"— so that in Christ Jesus the blessing of Abraham might come to the Gentiles, so that we might receive the promised Spirit through faith."*

And verses 28-29 go on to explain:

> *"There is neither Jew nor Greek, there is neither slave nor free, there is no male and female, for you are all one in Christ Jesus. And if you are Christ's, then you are Abraham's offspring, heirs according to promise."*

Through Christ and by faith, we have access to the promises meant for Abraham and his offspring because we are now considered his offspring. Possessions should not be feared; just like everything else, we must keep them in perspective. 1 Timothy 6:6-10 (ESV) states:

> *"But godliness with contentment is great gain, for we brought nothing into the world, and we cannot take anything out of the world. But if we have food and clothing, with these we will be content. But those who*

> desire to be rich fall into temptation, into a snare, into many senseless and harmful desires that plunge people into ruin and destruction. For the love of money is a root of all kinds of evils. It is through this craving that some have wandered away from the faith and pierced themselves with many pangs."

Possessions are not inherently evil. They can be used to provide medicine, food, education, and even spread the gospel worldwide. Without finances, the work of God would stop. The key in this verse is the need to avoid being motivated by riches. Our main motivation needs to be doing the work God has assigned us to do, and when He blesses us in the process, continue the work assigned to us, or even use those finances to expand it, but not allow them to change us or what we are all about. God is the source of those blessings, and He should always remain at the center of our lives. Deuteronomy 8:18 (ESV) admonishes us in this area, stating that:

> "You shall remember the LORD your God, for it is he who gives you power to get wealth, that he may confirm his covenant that he swore to your fathers, as it is this day."

When we start experiencing blessings, let's remember where the blessings came from in the first place. Not to feel guilty or unworthy, but to remain humble so that God can continue to pour unto us His blessings. 1 John 2:15-17 (ESV) states:

> "Do not love the world or the things in the world. If anyone loves the world, the love of the Father is not in him. For all that is in the world—the desires of the flesh and the desires of the eyes and pride of life—is not from the Father but is from the world. And the world is passing away along with its desires, but whoever does the will of God abides forever."

One last point I'd like to add is that God sometimes will test our hearts by blessing us with material possessions. Luke 16:11

(ESV) states: *"If then you have not been faithful in the unrighteous wealth, who will entrust to you the true riches?"* If we are faithful with material possessions, He can trust us with Spiritual possessions (true riches). By the same token, if we remain faithful to him with the possessions, he has entrusted us with, He will trust us with more responsibility and even more of those blessings (Matthew 25:23).

Questions to Reflect

Do I believe God wants to prosper me in every area?

___

Am I committed to remaining faithful to Him once He blesses me abundantly?

___

Will I give Him the Glory for all the victories in my life and use those resources to accomplish His purposes on earth?

___

Breakthrough Prayer

Thank you, Lord, for Your blessings so far and for the many blessings in every area that You will continue to pour into my life. Help me to acknowledge You at every turn, recognizing that You are the source of all those blessings, and without You, I cannot accomplish anything of true value. Use my prosperity and success to spread Your Kingdom unto others who need to hear Your truth. In Jesus' name. Amen

Day Sixteen

Jonah Received an Assignment from God
(Jonah 1:1-2)

Jonah's story starts when God called him to perform a difficult task:

"Now the word of the Lord came to Jonah the son of Amittai, saying, 'Arise, go to Nineveh, that great city, and call out against it, for their evil has come up before me'" (ESV, Jonah 1:1-2).

God commanded Jonah to go to the City of Nineveh, the capital of Assyria and "the most powerful city in the ancient Near East."[3] Its overwhelming greatness lasted about 150 years until 612 B.C. when they fell to the Babylonians and Medes."[4]

"But Jonah ran away from the Lord and headed for Tarshish. He went down to Joppa, where he found a ship bound for that port. After paying the fare, he went aboard and sailed for Tarshish to flee from the Lord" (ESV, Jonah 1:3).

God instructed him to journey to Nineveh, but Jonah did the contrary of what God had asked him to do. He veered off course towards Joppa, purchased a ticket, and fled in a ship headed to Tarshish, situated on the coast of the Mediterranean Sea, in the opposite direction.

Why Did Jonah Run Away?

Jonah's uncharacteristic silence toward God during this time was unexpected.[10] He didn't even question God; instead, he boldly took action in the opposite direction. But why? Up until this point, Jonah had been a faithful servant of God. The Book of 2 Kings, recounts an episode where Jonah delivered a prophetic message to King Jeroboam II:

"He [Jeroboam II] was the one who restored the boundaries of Israel from Lebo Hamath to the Dead Sea, in accordance with the word of the Lord, the God of Israel, spoken through his servant Jonah son of Amittai, the prophet from Gath Hepher" (ESV, 2 Kings 14:25).

The initial response of many readers is to oversimplify this story, quickly passing judgment on Jonah and reducing the entire book to the lesson of "not doing what Jonah did." However, the story goes deeper than that. The crucial question is the motivation behind Jonah's blunt rebellion. He decisively chose to avoid his assignment and flee in the opposite direction. What was it about this task that he found so objectionable? Scripture indicates Jonah was fleeing "from the Lord," implying a personal conflict with God over this commission.[11] But what precisely sparked this conflict?

Scholars highlight several reasons why Jonah chose to disobey and flee. One such reason is his fear of the Assyrians, given their long history of violence. Additionally, Jonah may have feared being labeled a "false prophet" and facing death if the prophecy remained unfulfilled. This fear would persist even if the people repented and God withheld judgment; while some might be grateful, others could turn against Jonah, doubting his authenticity. While these factors hold validity, the deeper layers of the story tie back to the intricate history between the Assyrians and the Israelites.

Israel-Assyria Conflict

The Assyrians had long been regarded as one of Israel's persistent adversaries. Nineveh, known as the "evil capital of the Assyrian nation," housed an estimated population of around 120,000 during Jonah's era (3:3; 4:11). Situated in present-day northern Iraq, across the Tigris River from the modern city of Mosul, Nineveh boasted opulence, with its grand palaces and lush gardens. It stood as a prominent hub for the Assyrian military, serving as a critical training ground for troops.

Throughout history, the Assyrian empire posed a continual threat to Israel, a reality that persisted before and after Jonah's time. However, during Jonah's era, a rare period of peace spanned approximately ten years.[16]

They would frequently launch attacks on Israel and Judah, devastating the countryside and capturing inhabitants. Assyria employed torture and mutilation as political tools to deter potential adversaries. Renowned for their formidable charioteers, Assyrian reliefs portray chariots manned by two to four armed soldiers. Upon conquering a city, they were notorious for subjecting captives to brutal torture. Consequently, they were "feared and hated."[18] Isaiah 52:4 (**NKJV**) gives reference to the relationship of Israel with Assyria:

For thus says the Lord GOD:

"My people went down at first
Into Egypt to dwell there;
Then the Assyrian oppressed them without cause".

Not long after Jonah's era, Assyria regained its status as a regional powerhouse. Approximately 30 years later, Shalmaneser V toppled the Northern Kingdom in 722 BC (referenced in 2 Kings 17:1-6 and 1 Chronicles 5:26). Jonah might have hesitated to share his message out of fear that if the people of Nineveh repented and were spared from destruction, they might retaliate by attacking his homeland in the future.[19] This concern wasn't unfounded, as history eventually confirmed.[20]

The nation of Assyria eventually became responsible for the destruction of Israel's capital city, Samaria, and the deportation of its population. This devastating event unfolded starting in 722 BC and reached its culmination during the reign of Sargon II (722-705 BC) when the capture was officially declared.[25] Records indicate that 27,290 Israelites were taken into captivity, and captives from Babylon and Syria were resettled in the conquered territory.[26]

Here's the account according to 2 Kings 18:10-12 (ESV):

> *"And at the end of three years they took it. In the sixth year of Hezekiah, that is, the ninth year of Hoshea king of Israel, Samaria was taken. Then the king of Assyria carried Israel away captive to Assyria, and put them in Halah and by the Habor, the River of Gozan, and in the cities of the Medes, because they did not obey the voice of the LORD their God, but transgressed His covenant and all that Moses the servant of the LORD had commanded; and they would neither hear nor do them."*

Israel was caught off guard by the Assyrian attacks at that juncture. Enjoying a period of political and military triumph, they focused on fortifying their northern border. Meanwhile, Assyria was engrossed in conflicts with their northern adversaries, particularly the Urartu Mountain tribes of Urartu, leading them into a sense of misplaced assurance.

Life Lesson # 16:
Disobedience: An Open Door

Highlighting the significance of Israel's lack of wholehearted devotion to the Lord, it's crucial to note that their adversaries were permitted to prevail over them. This recurring pattern is evident throughout the Old Testament, underscoring the potential for apprehension regarding their enemies' looming threat of destruction. It's essential to understand that God did not desire their enemies' triumph; Israel's actions facilitated it. God had pledged protection to those who adhered to and obeyed His commandments. In Deuteronomy 28:7 (ESV), the Lord assured Israel of safeguarding and triumph over their adversaries:

> *"The LORD will grant that the enemies who rise up against you will be defeated before you. They will come at you from one direction but flee from you in seven."*

This is something that applies to us as well. As long as we are walking in the will of God, we are under His umbrella of protection and have nothing to fear. Psalm 91 (ESV) reminds us of this when it says:

> *"Whoever dwells in the shelter of the Most High*
> *will rest in the shadow of the Almighty.*
> *I will say of the LORD, 'He is my refuge and my fortress,*
> *my God, in whom I trust.'*
> *Surely he will save you*
> *from the fowler's snare*
> *and from the deadly pestilence.*
> *He will cover you with his feathers,*
> *and under his wings you will find refuge;*

his faithfulness will be your shield and rampart.
You will not fear the terror of night,
nor the arrow that flies by day,
nor the pestilence that stalks in the darkness,
nor the plague that destroys at midday.
A thousand may fall at your side,
ten thousand at your right hand,
but it will not come near you.
You will only observe with your eyes
and see the punishment of the wicked."

The good news is that God is merciful and grants us grace, forgiveness, and restoration when we repent wholeheartedly. In 2 Chronicles 7:13-15 (ESV), the Lord promises to come to the rescue when the people repent:

"When I shut up the heavens so that there is no rain, or command the locust to devour the land, or send pestilence among my people, if my people who are called by my name humble themselves, and pray and seek my face and turn from their wicked ways, then I will hear from heaven and will forgive their sin and heal their land. Now my eyes will be open and my ears attentive to the prayer that is made in this place."

The Lord expects us to follow His ways as a requirement for blessings. When we walk according to God's will for us, He backs us up; He grants us provision, protection, favor, and victory. When we walk according to the flesh, we then open the door to the enemy:

"Therefore, having put away falsehood, let each one of you speak the truth with his neighbor, for we are members one of another. Be angry and do not sin; do not let the sun go down on your anger, and give no opportunity to the devil. Let the thief no longer steal, but rather let him labor, doing

honest work with his own hands, so that he may have something to share with anyone in need. Let no corrupting talk come out of your mouths, but only such as is good for building up, as fits the occasion, that it may give grace to those who hear. And do not grieve the Holy Spirit of God, by whom you were sealed for the day of redemption. Let all bitterness and wrath and anger and clamor and slander be put away from you, along with all malice. Be kind to one another, tenderhearted, forgiving one another, as God in Christ forgave you" (ESV, Ephesians 4:25-32).

Notice how it specifically says, "Give no opportunity to the devil." The devil does not have a right in our lives as long as we walk in the Spirit. It is not the will of God for us to be oppressed by the devil. We must refuse to engage in those practices that open the door to the enemy. James 4:7-10 (ESV) states:

"Submit yourselves therefore to God. Resist the devil, and he will flee from you. Draw near to God, and he will draw near to you. Cleanse your hands, you sinners, and purify your hearts, you double-minded. Be wretched and mourn and weep. Let your laughter be turned to mourning and your joy to gloom. Humble yourselves before the Lord, and he will exalt you."

Notice that this Scripture does not command us to pray for long hours or do an entire course on deliverance to be set free, but to "submit to God" and then "resist the devil," these are actions that we have control over. If we make the right choice, the devil has no more foothold in our lives. He has to flee. That's how much authority we have when we are surrendered or submitted to God.

Questions to Reflect

Are there any areas of my life where I have left an open door for the enemy to come in?

_____

_____

_____

Am I willing to repent and close those doors once and for all today?

_____

_____

_____

Breakthrough Prayer

Dear Lord, I submit myself to you. Please show me every open door in my life that might allow the enemy to come in and disrupt my life in any way. Show me if I'm involved with relationships that are harmful to me or any other aspect of my life that might not be adding to what you have called me to do. Help me to close those doors today and never to open them back up again. Please forgive me for every sin in my life and help me live a life that is truly surrendered to you. Thank You that as I follow your will, your Word says that I have authority over the devil, and he must flee. I resist him today and declare that anything that he had attempted against my life is now void, and every work of the devil against my life and my family, up until this point, is broken in Jesus' name. I am free to serve you! I am free to live for you! In Jesus' name. Amen.

Day Seventeen

Why Did Jonah Disobey?

As of a week ago (October 2023), Israel has been under attack from Hamas. Hamas, identified as a terrorist group, perpetrated heinous acts, including the kidnapping of innocent Israeli women, children, and older adults. Reports indicate atrocities such as the beheading of infants and the slaughter and torture of thousands of civilians. This shocking terrorist assault has elicited worldwide condemnation. There is unequivocally no justification for these actions; they epitomize pure evil. Such appalling acts are antithetical to any divine intent; they defy the very notion of God's benevolence. As John 10:10 (ESV) states:

> "The thief comes only to steal and kill and destroy; I have come that they may have life, and have it to the full."

The thief is the devil, and he is behind these actions. Please make no mistake about it. The pain, loss of life, and devastation caused by these events are beyond words. There are no adequate descriptors for the magnitude of what has unfolded.

We can understand Jonah's perspective in light of these horrific current events. Having grown up in Israel, he would have been exposed to the tales of atrocities committed by the Assyrians against his people. Jonah's father hailed from Gath Hepher, a village three miles northeast of Nazareth. Thus, Jonah was intimately acquainted with the havoc the Assyrians had inflicted upon Israel over the years.[25]

Some argue that Jonah was fearful for his life. However, when the Lord called Jonah, Assyria's power diminished,[26] and several decades passed without antagonism towards Israel. It could be argued that fear played a role, but as we will explore, it was likely not the only reason since he demonstrated bravery by risking his life to save the pagan sailors. If fear wasn't the primary cause of his rebellion, what was it?

Jonah was among the select Old Testament prophets, including Nahum and Obadiah, whom God called to preach to the Gentiles.[27] In the Old Testament, prophets were primarily sent to convey messages to the Israelites. Accustomed to being God's chosen people, they may not have felt inclined to reach out to those beyond their community. From an Israelite perspective, the expectation was that God's grace would be reserved solely for them as the chosen ones, while the Assyrians of Nineveh were often viewed with contempt.[28]

With that backdrop in mind, it becomes evident that God's assignment to Jonah directly contradicted his culture and his people's prevailing beliefs and conduct. However, this was not aligned with God's intended treatment of other nations. From the outset, God's plan for Israel was to be a blessing to all nations. In Genesis 12:1-3 (ESV), God spoke to Abraham, the Father of the nation of Israel, and said:

> «*Go from your country, your people, and your Father›s household to the land I will show you.*
> "*I will make you into a great nation,*
> *and I will bless you;*
> "*I will make your name great,*
> *and you will be a blessing.*
> "*I will bless those who bless you,*
> *and whoever curses you I will curse;*
> *and all peoples on earth*
> *will be blessed through you.*»

In Exodus 19:5-6, God called the people of Israel to obedience so they could fulfill their role as a "Kingdom of Priests." Israel was referred to as God's "firstborn son" (Exodus 4:22). Throughout history, it's evident that God's intention was to extend salvation and the knowledge of Himself to all nations, not solely to the Israelites. He intended to utilize Israel as the instrument for this mission, a mission that would ultimately find its fullest expression with the arrival of Jesus, the Messiah. Unfortunately, the Israelites had become complacent within their community.

Some scholars would concur that this story raises awareness of "Jewish hostility towards Gentiles"[29] and aims to "depict the pagan sailors and the Ninevites in a positive manner."[30] This theme later resurfaced in the reforms of Ezra and Nehemiah.[31]

Jonah finally talked to God and clarified his reasons for fleeing; he admitted that he had sought refuge in Tarshish because he understood God's compassionate nature: "gracious, merciful, slow to anger, and abounding in steadfast love, relenting from disaster" (4:2b). Jonah feared that if the Assyrians repented, God would show them mercy, a prospect he fervently opposed. In his view, they were undeserving of such leniency, having long posed a threat to Israel. Jonah's actions stemmed from his deep concern for Israel's well-being, viewing Nineveh's potential future role through the lens of its troubled past.[33] These motives seemed reasonable to him.

Life Lesson # 17:
Social Constructs Above God's Direction

If God knew Jonah's background and the tense history between Israel and Assyria, why did He select Jonah for the task? For example, why not choose someone from Assyria to warn about their sin? Given God's knowledge of the complex relationship between Israel and

Assyria and Jonah's personal history and reservations, the decision to pick him seems odd.

The answer may very well lie in God's multifaceted intentions. Not only was He concerned about the salvation of the Assyrians, but He also aimed to instruct Jonah and Israel. Through this mission, God was actively working on Jonah's heart and revealing His compassion toward foreign nations—a sentiment not widely embraced in ancient Israel. This assignment was designed to challenge and dismantle Jonah and Israel's deeply ingrained cultural biases, fostering a broader understanding of God's inclusive love and mercy.

This "deep-seated" wrong belief system can be present in any of us and is described as a "stronghold" in 2 Corinthians 10:4 (ESV): *"The weapons we fight with are not the weapons of the world. On the contrary, they have divine power to demolish strongholds."*

When God issues a command, His interest extends beyond mere compliance; He delves into the depths of our intentions. Our hesitation to obey often reveals underlying strongholds or wrong belief systems requiring attention. These may manifest as fear, bitterness, or unforgiveness, or perhaps as a scarcity mindset or unbelief. Whatever the issue, once brought into the light, we can achieve lasting victory over it. Once we are set free from bondage, we can emulate God more closely and fulfill His purposes. God's intention in exposing these issues isn't to condemn or shame us but to facilitate our journey towards greater likeness to Him. Jesus clarified this concept in John 8:31-36 (ESV):

> *"So Jesus said to the Jews who had believed him, 'If you abide in my word, you are truly my disciples, and you will know the truth, and the truth will set you free.' They answered him, 'We are offspring of Abraham and have never been enslaved to anyone. How is it that you say, "You will become free?"' Jesus answered them, 'Truly, truly, I say to you, everyone who practices sin is a slave to sin. The slave does not*

remain in the house forever; the son remains forever. So, if the Son sets you free, you will be free indeed.'"

Jesus desires to liberate us from sin and anything hindering our complete obedience to God. Jonah's disobedience blatantly revealed his indifference towards the people of Nineveh. Despite knowing that their fate hung in the balance and that, without warning, they faced destruction, Jonah's concern was exclusively focused on his nation and his interests. His actions also laid bare a deeper unforgiveness issue bordering on hatred. According to Ezekiel 3:18-19, when God entrusts a prophet with a warning for wicked people and fails to deliver it, the prophet bears responsibility for their destruction.

Jonah's attitude found validation within his social circles; it is deemed "understandable" within his context and, unfortunately, echoes ideas prevalent in today's society. However, it contradicts the very essence of God's compassion and love for humanity. God desires us to mirror His boundless love for others, irrespective of their actions towards us or societal norms. Forgiveness, mercy, and unconditional love define the God we worship; through these virtues, we reflect the true essence of who He is.

God's love extends to all nations. His overarching plan, established from the outset, encompasses blessings for every corner of the earth (Genesis 12:3). Isaiah was granted a vision by the Lord, portraying a united gathering of nations, including Israel's adversaries, converging to worship Him (Isaiah 19:23-25). This principle finds manifestation in the Gospels, exemplified particularly in Matthew 8:5-13. Here, Jesus highlights the centurion's faith and prophesies the inclusion of countless Gentiles, coming from "the east and the west," who will partake in the kingdom of heaven alongside Abraham, Isaac, and Jacob (Matthew 8:11), illustrating God's inclusive love for all peoples.[34]

Jesus continually confronted the customs and traditions of Israel head-on. Whether it was through the parable of the "good Samaritan"

(Luke 10), His encounter with the woman at the well (John 4), His interactions with Mary (John 12), His healing on the Sabbath, or His welcoming embrace of children, Jesus fearlessly challenged the prevailing cultural norms of His time. He courageously exposed any constructs that contradicted God's will, regardless of whether it offended the social elites.

How often do we pause to scrutinize specific attitudes or social practices that stray from God's heart? Even within the church, do we sincerely contemplate what actions Jesus would take or whom He would associate with? Romans 12:2 underscores this critical reflection and offers us a blueprint for achieving it:

Do not conform to the pattern of this world, but be transformed by the renewing of your mind. Then you will be able to test and approve what God's will is—his good, pleasing and perfect will.

As we delve deeper into the story of Jonah, we will notice that God's expectations of us remain firm regardless of cultural influences. He holds us to higher standards and calls us to live up to them, irrespective of the sacrifices involved. Ultimately, He rewards us based on our obedience to His standards, not society's.

We are not excused from doing what is righteous simply because our peers or families may disapprove. God has established high standards for us, but He has also empowered us to live up to them through the Baptism of the Holy Spirit and anointing (see more on this at the end of the book). God is our ultimate standard, and we are tasked with renewing our minds through His Word to discern and obediently follow His flawless will for our lives.

Questions to Reflect

What areas of my life did God highlight as I was reading?

_____
_____
_____

Are there specific people that I desire to please above God?

_____
_____
_____

Am I willing to make the changes in the areas that God is showing me so that I can fully please Him and live the life of victory He has planned for me?

_____
_____
_____

Breakthrough Prayer

Thank you, Lord, for giving me the power to live a life that follows your standards instead of this culture. Reveal any areas of compromise in which I may be following the standards of my culture or my idea of what's best instead of what You want. Set me free from any stronghold that may be keeping me in bondage to this way of life. I want my heart, mind, emotions, and walk to align with You and who You want me to be. Thank You for the victory. In Jesus' name. Amen.

Day Eighteen

Jonah's Journey Away from His Calling (Jonah 1:4-16)

Jonah fled, seeking to evade God's daunting assignment for his life. The task was not merely difficult due to the relentless nature of the people involved but also because it contradicted the narrative ingrained in him throughout his upbringing.

Yet, despite Jonah's attempt to escape, God did not abandon him. Nor did He pass judgment, but instead showed mercy. Out of His profound love for Jonah, God orchestrated a sequence of events to capture his attention and guide him back onto the correct course. As Hebrews 12:5-11 (ESV) explains:

> "And have you completely forgotten this word of encouragement that addresses you as a father addresses his son? It says,
> "My son, do not make light of the Lord's discipline,
> and do not lose heart when he rebukes you,
> because the Lord disciplines the one he loves,
> and he chastens everyone he accepts as his son.
> "Endure hardship as discipline; God is treating you as his children. For what children are not disciplined by their father? If you are not disciplined—and everyone undergoes discipline—then you are not legitimate, not true sons and daughters at all. Moreover, we have all had human fathers who disciplined us and we respected them for it. How much more should we submit to the Father of spirits and live! They disciplined us for a little while as they thought best; but God disciplines

us for our good, in order that we may share in his holiness. No discipline seems pleasant at the time, but painful. Later on, however, it produces a harvest of righteousness and peace for those who have been trained by it."

God's love for us is infinite, manifested through His willingness to allow diverse circumstances into our lives. These aren't punishments but corrective actions aimed at guiding us back to the intended path. Ideally, our faithfulness to God's will would be voluntary, sparing us from the need for these severe interventions. Nevertheless, God allows these interventions out of His great mercy and love for us.

Initially, God employed the might of natural forces—a "great wind on the sea" and "a violent storm"—to capture Jonah's attention regarding his disobedience. Despite these dramatic signals, Jonah either failed to heed them or consciously chose to disregard God's call:

> *«Then the Lord sent a great wind on the sea, and such a violent storm arose that the ship threatened to break up. All the sailors were afraid and each cried out to his own God. And they threw the cargo into the sea to lighten the ship."*
> *Then, the Lord used the ship's captain, who went straight to Jonah and rebuked him.*
> *But Jonah had gone below deck, where he lay down and fell into a deep sleep. The captain went to him and said, "How can you sleep? Get up and call on your God! Maybe he will take notice of us so that we will not perish" (ESV, Jonah 1:4-6).*

Now Jonah was finally awake and aware of the danger of the situation, but there is no record that he cried out to God. So, the Lord used the sailors, who, out of desperation, cast lots to find the person responsible for this epic storm. They had enough sense to realize this storm was not natural but supernatural. When the lot fell on Jonah, the sailors started questioning him. They were being used to talk sense into Jonah:

> *"So they asked him, "Tell us, who is responsible for making all this trouble for us? What kind of work do you do? Where do you come from? What is your country? From what people are you?" (ESV, Jonah 1:8)*

Jonah finally spoke up. He confessed his identity, his faith, the identity of the God he served, and the fact that he was running away from God:

> *"He answered, "I am a Hebrew, and I worship the Lord, the God of heaven, who made the sea and the dry land."*
> *This terrified them and they asked, "What have you done?" (They knew he was running away from the Lord, because he had already told them so)" (ESV, Jonah 1:9-10).*

At this point, the sailors could connect the dots and concluded that Jonah had caused this storm by disobedience. They also realized that the storm would only calm if they did something. The sea was getting rougher and rougher. So they asked him, *"What should we do to you to make the sea calm down for us?"(ESV, Jonah 1:11)*

Jonah finally recognized that this was his fault and was willing to pay the penalty for his sin. He was ready to give up his life so that the sailors could live:

> *"Pick me up and throw me into the sea," he replied, "and it will become calm. I know that it is my fault that this great storm has come upon you" (ESV, Jonah 1:12).*

The men did not want to do this at first. It seemed like such a hefty price to pay. They tried other methods but had no success:

> *"Instead, the men did their best to row back to land. But they could not, for the sea grew even wilder than before" (ESV, Jonah 1:13).*

Finally, the sailors realized that their best efforts would not work, so they cried out to God first, something Jonah hadn't done yet, and decided to throw Jonah overboard:

> *"Then they cried out to the Lord, "Please, Lord, do not let us die for taking this man's life. Do not hold us accountable for killing an innocent man, for you, Lord, have done as you pleased." Then they took Jonah and threw him overboard and the raging sea grew calm" (ESV, Jonah 1:14-15).*

Once the men threw Jonah overboard, the sea grew calm almost instantly. This sign brought the fear of God to these sailors:

> *"At this the men greatly feared the Lord, and they offered a sacrifice to the Lord and made vows to him" (ESV, Jonah 1:16).*

The appropriate reaction from Jonah should have been immediate repentance and a willingness to comply with God's directive to journey to Nineveh.[35] However, Jonah's stubbornness persisted. Mirroring God's steadfastness towards His children, He never gave up on Jonah.

The sailors, reluctant to resort to drastic measures, attempted to navigate towards the shore instead of casting Jonah overboard. Yet, as the storm intensified beyond control, they found no alternative.

Life Lesson # 18:
Being Real but Improper vs. Fake and Proper

This part of the story brings to mind the biblical account of Jacob wrestling with God, leading to God changing his name to Israel (Genesis 32:22-32). Jonah and Jacob showed a similar determination to have their way and were unwilling to give up easily. Jonah was even prepared to sacrifice his life rather than fulfill God's assignment, while Jacob wrestled through the night to receive a blessing. In both instances, they exhibited relentlessness in their interactions with God, to which God responded.

Jesus illustrated this point with the parable of the persistent widow in Luke 18, where a judge granted her request simply due to her unyielding persistence. God values decisiveness, boldness, and resolve in His children. He desires authenticity, wanting to understand our true desires and thoughts, and He is not offended by our persistence; rather, He willingly engages with us in our journey of faith.

We shouldn't rush to judge Jonah for his actions. He took a stand, although we should recognize that it was foolish. His image of God and his view of his enemies led him to arrive at the wrong conclusion. Despite this, he genuinely believed he followed what was right, even when he opposed God's will.

In Jacob's story, God honored his stubbornness and perseverance to the extent that He changed Jacob's name to Israel following their night of wrestling. God respected Jacob's resilience and determination.

We are encouraged to be authentic and honest with God, sharing our true thoughts and feelings with Him. He desires this openness from us. Even if we are mistaken in our beliefs, He can take them and help us course correct. God values our sincerity and transparency. It's far better to engage with God truthfully, even if we are wrong, then to fake compliance!

God desires genuine relationships with His children. He welcomes hearing both the good and the bad, even when it might seem unconventional or contrary to religious norms. We can freely express ourselves to God about anything and everything. Although Jonah initially kept his thoughts from God, he eventually confided in the sailors and confirmed his feelings through his actions. Even if our actions and words veer in the wrong direction, they are preferable to remaining passive and silent. Revelation 3:15 (ESV) conveys a message from God to the church in Laodicea, emphasizing the importance of genuine engagement and sincerity:

> *"I know your works: you are neither cold nor hot. Would that you were either cold or hot! So, because you are lukewarm, and neither hot nor cold, I will spit you out of my mouth."*

I've always wondered why He'd favor someone cold over someone lukewarm; both are distant from him. Why does one hold more appeal? Reflecting on Jonah's story, it becomes clear that God prefers authenticity, even if it means someone like Jonah is going to extreme lengths, because God can intervene and enact change within their heart. A "lukewarm" individual might ignore God, going through the motions of "serving" and performing "religious rituals" while their heart remains disengaged. Hypocrisy turns others away from God.

Those individuals seek the approval of others. Jonah wasn't concerned with appearing religious; he was authentically honest, even with the sailors. He refused to obey God and deliberately chose to go in the opposite direction. In a sense, I believe God respects that. He can engage with an honest individual. Which kind of relationship would you prefer? One with a friend who pretends everything is fine or someone who communicates clearly, for better or worse? It might not always be smooth, but it fosters a healthy relationship built on mutual respect. When we act contrary to our true selves, pretending to deceive others and even God, we mock Him. It's disrespectful. He abhors such pretense. In Matthew 23:26-28 (ESV), Jesus denounced those who were insincere toward God and others, illustrating that God sees into the depths of each person.

> *"You blind Pharisee! First clean the inside of the cup and the plate, that the outside also may be clean. "Woe to you, scribes and Pharisees, hypocrites! For you are like whitewashed tombs, which outwardly appear beautiful, but within are full of dead people's bones and all uncleanness. So you also outwardly appear righteous to others, but within you are full of hypocrisy and lawlessness."*

God indeed values authenticity and honesty, even if it seems unconventional or "improper," over someone who merely appears religious but lacks integrity. This concept can be challenging to grasp in a society where the church often prioritizes traditions and appearances. There's been a tendency to focus more on outward impressions to outsiders rather than addressing internal imperfections and striving to please God. Hebrews 4:14-16 (ESV) underscores this principle:

> *"Seeing then that we have a great High Priest who has passed through the heavens, Jesus the Son of God, let us hold fast our confession. For we do not have a High Priest who cannot sympathize with our weaknesses, but was in all points tempted as we are, yet without sin. Let us therefore come boldly to the throne of grace, that we may obtain mercy and find grace to help in time of need."*

Jesus, having experienced life in a human body, understands our struggles intimately and can help us with our weaknesses. If we shy away from being direct and honest with Him about our desires and feelings, we limit His ability to help us effectively.

The pagan sailors, deeply affected by the incident, believed in and feared God. They offered sacrifices and vows to Him, recognizing His presence and power. Through this tumultuous storm, God communicated His concern for all nations, highlighting the significance of Nineveh in His eyes. Moreover, it underscored the value of Jonah's life, as God persistently pursued him despite his blatant disobedience. Yet, Jonah remained stubborn even amidst the imminent threat of death. The irony here is that while Jonah remained stubborn, the sailors from foreign lands demonstrated remarkable sensitivity to God, displaying greater faith and reverence than even His chosen prophet.

Questions to Reflect

Are there any aspects of who God is or how He operates that I tend to struggle with?

_____

_____

_____

Is there any specific instruction from God or assignment in my life that I have run away from or have not fully embraced yet?

_____

_____

_____

Have I been open to God about my reservations or whatever has kept me from diving head-on into His will for my life?

_____

_____

_____

Breakthrough Prayer

Thank you, Lord, for knowing everything about me. You created me and accepted me the way I am. Thank You for allowing me to come to You just as I am. Thank You for sympathizing with my struggles and being willing to make your power perfect in my weaknesses. Take my weaknesses, faults, and shortcomings and turn them into a testimony of your mercy, power, and grace. In Jesus' name. Amen.

Day Nineteen

Jonah's Desperate Moment (Jonah 1:17-2:9)

When Jonah was thrown into the sea, he reached his lowest point, with no hope of survival within the raging waters. He accepted his death as the inevitable fate that his own choices brought upon him. He had acknowledged his rebellion against God to the sailors and was prepared to face the consequences of his mistakes, even to the point of sacrificing his life for them.

His willingness to show love and sacrifice for the foreign sailors contrasted sharply with his deep-seated hatred towards the Ninevites. Jonah did not have a problem with all foreign nations, but the Assyrians were not on his good side. Despite his readiness to embrace pagan sailors, Jonah couldn't muster the same compassion for the people of Nineveh.

Jonah's Desperate Cry

Jonah's desperate cry reached God in an instant as he was sinking and on the brink of drowning. His prayer of thanksgiving and recommitment unfolded at some point during his dark 3-day journey within the belly of the great fish. Such prayers resonate throughout the Bible, similar to Jonah's. Psalms 86 and 88 stand as mere glimpses of this earnest prayer. They are prayers that spring up from the depths of the heart. They overflow with raw human emotion, unfiltered honesty, and a fervent desire that aligns with the essence of what God seeks in the prayers of His children.

Jonah's prayer begins with vividly depicting the moment he desperately cried out to God. As the sailors threw him overboard, he started sinking and was enveloped by the currents and waves, with his head entangled in seaweed. He felt as if he were descending to the very "roots of the mountains." His life was slipping away before his very eyes. He was trapped forever, doomed to spend eternity in hell, and any escape seemed impossible. It is then that he decided to call on the Lord. He could have done it when the Lord gave him this challenging assignment; he could have done it when the storm began in the ship or when the pagan sailors started questioning him. He had plenty of opportunities along the way, but he did not recognize them. It took Jonah to be standing face to face with death itself to finally reach out to God. It was not the most eloquent prayer, I can guarantee, nor the most appropriate place. But that was not an issue at all. This split second in time was a turning point in Jonah's life. He humbled himself and earnestly begged God for help, and God heard him.

Jonah's Immediate Answer to Prayer

It was at this moment, submerged in the dark depths of the stormy sea, that the first breakthrough in his story occurred:

> *"And the LORD designated a great fish to swallow Jonah, and Jonah was in the stomach of the fish for three days and three nights"* (NASB, Jonah 1:17).

Initially, one might assume the miracle lay in the fish that "saved" Jonah. However, the true miracle unfolded within Jonah's heart, which underwent a profound transformation. In his moment of despair, sinking into the depths, Jonah finally reached out to God. Despite feeling utterly lost and deeply entrenched in sin, Jonah's cry for help marked a pivotal shift in his life.

Right at that moment, Jonah may not have recognized the fish as an answer to his prayer. Although God responded promptly, the complete realization of His miracle didn't materialize until three days later. Remarkably, two miracles unfolded within that span. First, Jonah's life was spared, and second, his heart was transformed.

Gratefully, Jonah came to recognize that it was God who had dispatched the fish to rescue him. Despite his uncertainty about the duration of his ordeal and the uncertainty of survival, he acknowledged God's intervention. Instead of yielding to doubt or complaint, he chose to offer praise to God right there in the midst of that dark abyss:

> *"Then Jonah prayed to the LORD his God from the stomach of the fish, and he said,*
> *"I called out of my distress to the LORD,*
> *And He answered me.*
> *I called for help from the depth of Sheol;*
> *You heard my voice.*
> *For You threw me into the deep,*
> *Into the heart of the seas,*
> *And the current flowed around me.*
> *All Your breakers and waves passed over me"* (NASB, Jonah 2:1-3).

Jonah found himself sinking as he cried out for help.

> *"So I said, 'I have been cast out of Your sight.*
> *Nevertheless I will look again toward Your holy temple.*
> *Water encompassed me to the [d]point of death.*
> *The deep flowed around me,*

Seaweed was wrapped around my head.
I descended to the base of the mountains.
The earth with its bars was around me forever,
But You have brought up my life from the pit, LORD my God" *(Jonah 2:4-6).*

It appeared as though Jonah was nearing the bottom of the ocean, his life hanging in the balance:

"While I was fainting away,
I remembered the LORD,
And my prayer came to You,
Into Your holy temple
Those who are followers of worthless idols
Abandon their faithfulness,
But I will sacrifice to You
With a voice of thanksgiving.
That which I have vowed I will pay.
Salvation is from the LORD" (Jonah 2:7-9).

This serves as a powerful reminder that no matter how terrible our circumstances or how far we've strayed, God is both capable and eager to orchestrate a turnaround the instant we sincerely turn to Him. As Jonah descended, his heart shifted, perhaps in a fleeting moment of silent desperation beneath the waves. Yet, it proved enough for God to extend His saving grace.

> **...no matter how terrible our circumstances or how far we've strayed, God is both capable and eager to orchestrate a turnaround the instant we sincerely turn to Him.**

While dwelling within the confines of the fish, pondering upon God's miraculous rescue, he resolved to reaffirm his commitment to

God. He was determined to fulfill the promises he had made to the Lord. As Romans 2:4b rightly reminds us, *"God's kindness is meant to lead you to repentance."* Jonah experienced God's mercy and kindness firsthand. Despite his disobedience, God intervened. In response, Jonah determined to confront the challenging assignment he had been running away from.

Life Lesson # 19:
We Have the Answer as Soon as We Ask

Sometimes, when we earnestly pray for a breakthrough or a miracle, the answer arrives promptly, though unexpectedly. It's as if the solution is right before our eyes, yet it requires unfolding. The miracle is already in motion; it's merely a matter of it gradually taking shape.

By faith, what we pray for is already granted when we initially ask God, provided we ask with unwavering faith. Even though God answers our prayers, sometimes He begins by orchestrating events behind the scenes, dealing with our heart or any other aspect of the issue, so that His answer can be unfolded in a comprehensive manner. Occasionally, a spiritual battle may ensue, causing a delay in receiving our answer. Nevertheless, rest assured, our answer is on its way. As stated in 1 John 5:14-15 (**NASB**):

> *"This is the confidence which we have before Him, that, if we ask anything according to His will, He hears us. And if we know that He hears us in whatever we ask, we know that we have the requests which we have asked from Him."*

And Jesus said in John 16:23-24 (**NASB**):

"Truly, truly I say to you, if you ask the Father for anything in My name, He will give it to you. Until now you have asked for nothing in My name; ask and you will receive, so that your joy may be made full."

No matter how far we have run away from the Lord, He is willing and able to rescue us right where we are. He is right here, waiting for us to call on him. He has an answer for every prayer, a solution for every problem, and can make a way when there seems to be no way. Psalm 145:18-19 (NASB) states:

*"The LORD is near to all who call on Him,
To all who call on Him in truth.
He will fulfill the desire of those who fear Him;
He will also hear their cry for help and save them."*

We are never too far gone for God to take us back and place us right where we need to be.

Questions to Reflect

Which areas of my life do I need a miracle from God? Finances? Health? Relationships? Ministry?

_____

_____

_____

Have I opened up to God about it?

_____

_____

_____

Do I believe that the answer is on its way?

_____

_____

_____

Breakthrough Prayer

Thank you, Lord, for loving me and going to great lengths to lead me back on the right path. Please help me in every area where I feel stuck, frustrated, or lost. Help me come to You for everything, knowing You hear me. Make a way where there seems to be no way. Please open my eyes so that I can see the answer you've already placed in front of me. Thank You for being here. Thank You for hearing when I call on you. In Jesus' name. Amen.

Day Twenty

Jonah's Miracle (Jonah 2:10)

In Jonah's most desperate moment, he cried out to God. He humbled himself, acknowledging God for who He was, and in response, the Lord paved the way to his rescue—a unique, supernatural, and unexpected path custom-made for Jonah in a manner only God could orchestrate.

> *"Then the LORD commanded the fish, and it vomited Jonah up onto the dry land"* (NASB. Jonah 2:10).

Personal Story: God Brought Me back to the United States Against All Odds

Back in 2011, I lost my job and had to move back to Argentina (I'll go into more detail on day 27). I do believe that the Lord was dealing with me, and in hindsight, I am so glad I moved back at that point! However, after about 8 months of being there, the Lord started speaking to me about returning to the United States. I remember reasoning that if I hadn't been able to find a job with a visa while in the US, being in another country would only make that task impossible. That Sunday my local Pastor was teaching on the story of Peter and Jesus when he had been fishing all night and had caught nothing:

"Now when He had finished speaking, He said to Simon, "Put out into the deep water and let down your nets for a catch." Simon responded and said, "Master, we worked hard all night and caught nothing, but I will do as You say and let down the nets." And when they had done this, they caught a great quantity of fish, and their nets began to tear;" (NASB, Luke 5:4-6).

Through that story, the Lord showed me that it is not our effort alone that gets us the victory but the work that we put, following His command. Not everything we do will succeed, but when He commands us to do something and we do it, that's when we have the guaranteed victory. At that point we need to take action, because we will not fail!

With this teaching in mind, I decided to obey the Lord against all logic. I not only applied to every job I could think of, contacted everyone I knew, and sent them my resume, but I also renewed my passport, canceled my current lease on my apartment, and got ready to move back to the US in faith. His Word, plus action on our part, is what produces the results. They go hand in hand. As soon as everything was aligned, I received an email from my former boss saying that their bookkeeper had just resigned and asked if I could be there to start the job in 2 weeks. I then got them to sign the legal paperwork to show at the Embassy interview, and the same day I received the stamped passport in the mail, I got on a flight back to the US. Once the Lord finished the work He needed to accomplish in my heart through this specific season, He didn't just make a way for me to come back, but He did it fast! Likewise, when Jonah repented and made a decision to obey God, He not only saved Him, but He restored his Ministry right away!

> **His Word, plus action on our part, is what produces the results. They go hand in hand.**

Jonah's Second Chance (Jonah 3:1-3)

"Now the word of the LORD came to Jonah the second time, saying, "Arise, go to Nineveh, the great city, and proclaim to it the proclamation which I am going to tell you" (NASB, Jonah 3:1-2).

God accepted Jonah's apology and the renewal of his commitment, promptly issuing a new directive for him to proceed to Nineveh and deliver a message ordained by God. When we dedicate our lives to God, He holds us accountable, necessitating tangible actions to follow through on our commitment. It's comparable to accepting a job offer; our new employer anticipates our presence on Monday, ready to begin work diligently. Similarly, Jonah found himself immediately on "prophet duty" following his expulsion onto dry land by the fish. There was no delay allowed.

Reflecting on the journey of Jonah, I wonder whether the three days spent within the belly of the fish were the time it took the great fish to travel to the coast towards Nineveh. It's crucial to recall that Jonah initially boarded a ship bound for Tarsus, a route opposite to Nineveh. Yet, in God's kindness, the fish was directed to deposit him on the proper shore, facilitating his direct path to Nineveh on foot to deliver the divine message. This entailed several days of arduous travel, but the Lord ensured Jonah's alignment with his purpose. When God issues a command, it's not without its challenges; effort is required, yet He paves the way for us to fulfill it. Though intimidating, with his help and assistance, the impossible turns into possible.

God's second command to Jonah served as a sign of acceptance of his apology, and Jonah's swift obedience was his unequivocal response:

"So Jonah got up and went to Nineveh according to the word of the LORD. Now Nineveh was an exceedingly large city, a three days' walk" (NASB, Jonah 3:3).

Jonah's prayer and subsequent obedience were external displays of his repentance. While God hears our prayers, He observes our actions, which mirror our hearts.

Life Lesson #20:
God Makes a Way

When faced with a Desperate Situation, our instinct is often to rely solely on our natural senses, seeking solutions within the realm of our understanding. Sometimes, we may even find ourselves offering God our "suggestions" or "ideas" to navigate the situation and help us. However, it's essential to recognize that this isn't how He operates. God's power transcends our comprehension, and He orchestrates solutions in ways far beyond our imagination. As the God of the impossible, He doesn't require our input; instead, He manifests paths where there aren't any. His capabilities exceed our wildest expectations, and His answers surpass what we could ask or anticipate (Ephesians 3:20).

Attempting to rationalize the methods by which He will intervene overlooks His desire to surprise us with unique ways of doing things. As Isaiah 43:19 (**NASB**) affirms:

> *"Behold, I am going to do something new,*
> *Now it will spring up;*
> *Will you not be aware of it?*
> *I will even make a roadway in the wilderness,*
> *Rivers in the desert."*

God's creativity shines brightly in His interventions throughout history. It's a testament to God's inventive nature and His tailor-made plan for each individual's life.

God demonstrated remarkable creativity in delivering His people from slavery, in sending Jesus for our salvation, and in communicating His messages to humanity. Jesus consistently surprised people with His diverse approaches, whether in healing or providing for others, exhibiting a versatility that defied predictability.

Indeed, God's creativity extends to each individual's life as He crafts a distinctive plan for each person's journey. Your breakthrough, tailored to your unique circumstances, awaits as you wholeheartedly trust and surrender to His guidance. By placing your faith in Him and yielding to His divine plans, God faithfully orchestrates steps toward your breakthrough, guiding you with precision along the way.

Questions to Consider

Am I facing a situation where there seems to be no way out?

_____
_____
_____

Am I trying to solve my problems with logic, or am I resting in God's ability to provide a solution?

_____
_____
_____

Breakthrough Prayer

Thank you, Lord, for your incredible love and mercy on me. Please forgive me for any sin in my life and turn every situation that I am struggling with around. Make a supernatural path where there seems to be no way out. Open my eyes to see the way You are making for me and help me take steps towards my breakthrough. Thank you. I don't necessarily have to understand how You will come through for me; I must trust Your will! Make the crooked path straight and restore my life to reflect the blessed life You have designed for those who love and follow You. I love You. My life is Yours. In Jesus' name. Amen!

Day Twenty-one

Jonah's Message and Nineveh's Response (Jonah 3:4-10)

"Then Jonah began to go through the city one day's walk; and he cried out and said, "Forty more days, and Nineveh will be overthrown" (NASB, Jonah 3:4).

Israel wasn't the only nation with prophets; most countries boasted their own "prophets" who claimed to speak on behalf of their respective deities. The Assyrians, in particular, regarded prophets with significance, regardless of whether they represented their own gods or not. This was particularly evident during this period, as the Assyrians contended with considerable hardships, which they likely interpreted as divine punishment. The profound economic and political turmoil, coupled with a famine and a notable total solar eclipse in June of 763 BC, tarnished the reputation of the Assyrian gods.[37]

Background on Assyria

Let's take a step back to delve into the historical backdrop of Israel and Assyria, providing context to grasp the narrative better.

Nineveh served as the capital of the Assyrian empire during its final decades. Sennacherib (reigned 704-681 BCE) established it as his capital, as documented in 2 Kings 19:36. However, in 612 BCE, it succumbed to the forces of the Medes and Babylonians. The city faced divine judgment, as foretold in Zephaniah 2:13 and Nahum 3:7. The book of Jonah emphasizes Nineveh's greatness, mentioning it as "great" fourteen times, highlighting its political significance, vast size, and large population. Despite its grandeur, Nineveh was also characterized as wicked, drawing parallels to the sinful cities of Sodom and Gomorrah.

Roughly 150 years before Jonah's time (circa 883-824 BC), Assyria underwent a period of remarkable growth and prosperity, regarded as one of the golden ages of Mesopotamian history. However, in 826 BC, the nation began to falter, facing a significant rebellion that persisted for nearly seven years. Over the subsequent 70 years following this upheaval, Assyria entered a phase of decline, only to see a turnaround several decades later during the reign of King Tiglath-Pileser II (745-727 BC).

During this period of decline, a notable feature was the rise of influential provincial governors who functioned as de facto monarchs within their respective districts, acknowledging the authority of the King of Assyria while autonomously governing their regions. This era was characterized by reduced military campaigns against foreign nations, indicating either the weakened state or Assyria's internal turmoil. Consequently, Assyria refrained from launching any military offensives against Israel for nearly a decade, reflecting its diminished capacity or internal challenges hindering its military.

Additional factors contributing to the tumultuous era in Assyria encompassed a famine striking the land in 765 BC, possibly recurring in 759 BC or persisting throughout the entire seven-year span. There also was an earthquake, a sign of divine wrath, and a significant total solar eclipse, recorded on June 15, 763 BC. This likely instilled apprehension and fear among the populace of Assyria, further exacerbating the already troubled times. Solar eclipses were also viewed as signs of judgment and total solar eclipses are the rarest ones, happening approximately every 400 years. Moreover, this total solar eclipse happened at the time when Jonah gave the Word (either right before or right after).

God Orchestrated the Universe for This Very Moment

The combination of these catastrophic situations and the tumultuous times the nations have been enduring, coupled with the timing of this total solar eclipse, made for the perfect environment for Nineveh to be receptive to the prophet's warning and respond with such drastic measures. (Notice how God had accounted for Jonah's time of rebellion when He called him to go. Jonah arrived on the scene right on time for his assignment.)

Although they were unfamiliar with the God of Israel, they had gleaned some understanding of His mercy and were determined to take whatever steps necessary to appease Him.[38] They were desperate and prepared to turn to the true, living God for help. This readiness led the Assyrians to be receptive to the Word of the Lord through the prophet Jonah.

The timing couldn't have been more favorable. Because Jonah was a foreigner with nothing to gain by their repentance, this must have given his message even more credibility. Jonah wasn't seeking anything in return; on the contrary, he was taking a considerable risk. It was illogical for him to be there. This is comparable to a missionary leaving the comfort of his home country to preach the message of salvation in a dangerous territory. The message becomes even more trustworthy due to the sacrifice made to be able to deliver it.

One crucial point is that Jonah never mentioned the possibility of repentance or that God was willing to forgive them and relent from judgment. The message was clear: the city was destined for capture and ruin within 40 days. The symbolism of the number 40 represents grace, implying that although not explicitly stated, God was offering them a warning and a "grace period."

They were wise enough to believe in the Word of God and repent, hoping that He would relent from punishment:

> *"Then the people of Nineveh believed in God; and they called a fast and put on sackcloth, from the greatest to the least of them. When the word reached the king of Nineveh, he got up from his throne, removed his robe from himself, covered himself with sackcloth, and sat on the dust. And he issued a proclamation, and it said, "In Nineveh by the decree of the king and his nobles: No person, animal, herd, or flock is to taste anything. They are not to eat, or drink water. But every person and animal must be covered with sackcloth; and people are to call on God vehemently, and they are to turn, each one from his evil way, and from the violence which is in their hands. Who knows, God may turn and relent, and turn from His burning anger so that we will not perish"* (NASB, Jonah 3:5-9).

Once again, in this story, the people responded to God through actions. Their actions demonstrated their belief in God and their remorse for their sins, showing their willingness to turn away from them. They declared a nationwide fast, abstaining from food and water, including every member of society, even the animals. The king ordered everyone to clothe themselves in sackcloth and seek God's intervention. Fasting in the Old Testament was a common practice as a sign of mourning for sin, to elicit divine compassion or, at the very least, to mitigate divine wrath. Throughout the Old Testament, there are numerous references to fasting. It is essential to highlight that God did not view the mere absence of food as a genuine fast; it had to be accompanied by a change in behavior that aligned with God's values (Isaiah 58:3-7; Jeremiah 14:10-12; Zechariah 7-8).

The Ninevites, under the decree of their king, were instructed to not only observe the fast but also to renounce their wicked ways and violence. God then acknowledged their fast as legitimate. He responded to their humility and faith. It wasn't merely the act of fasting that pleased God, but rather the sincerity of their hearts.[40]

Life Lesson # 21:
An Entire Nation Can Be Saved

There are three different Greek words for the word "repentance" in the New Testament. One denotes a more emotional response or change of mind, but not a change of heart, like in the case of Judas (Mat 27:6), another one is "to change one's mind as a result of knowledge or information." The last one (metanoia) is used for true repentance, "a change of mind and purpose and life, to which remission of sin is promised."[52] The behavior change observed in Nineveh demonstrated this last type of repentance (Jonah 3:10).[41] In the New Testament, repentance and faith are closely intertwined (Acts 20:21). Jesus emphasized the importance of repentance to the Jews, stating, "Repent, for the kingdom of heaven is at hand" (Matthew 4:17), and commissioned his apostles to preach "repentance to all people."[42] In Acts 17:30-31 (NASB) we read:

> *"So having overlooked the times of ignorance, God is now proclaiming to mankind that all people everywhere are to repent, because He has set a day on which He will judge the world in righteousness through a Man whom He has appointed, having furnished proof to all people by raising Him from the dead."*

God wants us to repent for our own good, if not He would not even take the time to warn us. The King of Nineveh wisely concluded that 'the God who had warned of destruction proved to be a God of compassion.'[43]

God wanted them to repent, but He was also prepared to follow through with His warning if they did not repent. He keeps His Word. The Lord communicated this reality to the prophet Jeremiah, and it holds true for all nations without distinction:

Jeremiah 18:7-10 (NASB)

> *"At one moment I might speak concerning a nation or concerning a kingdom to uproot it, to tear it down, or to destroy it; if that nation against which I have spoken turns from its evil, I will relent of the disaster that I planned to bring on it. Or at another moment I might speak concerning a nation or concerning a kingdom to build up or to plant it; if it does evil in My sight by not obeying My voice, then I will relent of the good with which I said that I would bless it."*

The Lord's warnings, and promises, hinge on our responses. When we faithfully follow Him and act following His will, we can trust that His promises will be fulfilled. If we turn away from our sinful ways and earnestly seek His mercy, He can shield us from the most dreadful circumstances. This principle extends to all who call upon God. The Lord conveyed this message to King Solomon regarding his people:

> *"So although I wrote to you, it was not for the sake of the offender nor for the sake of the one offended, but that your earnestness in our behalf might be made known to you in the sight of God. Because of this, we have been comforted.*

> *"And besides our comfort, we rejoiced even much more for the joy of Titus, because his spirit has been refreshed by you all. For if I have boasted to him about you regarding anything, I was not put to shame. But as we*

spoke all things to you in truth, so also our boasting before Titus proved to be the truth" (NASB, 2 Chronicles 7:12-14).

God's pledge of compassion towards those who humble themselves, pray, and renounce their wickedness applies to individuals as much as it does to nations. The collective prayer and fasting hold immense value in God's eyes. No circumstance is beyond the scope of God's ability to redeem; His power can reverse even the most seemingly irreversible situations.

In the book of Genesis, there's a sad account where God contemplated judgment upon Sodom and Gomorrah due to their sinfulness. However, through Abraham's compelling and fervent prayer, he persuaded God to spare the cities if even ten righteous individuals were found within them:

"Then he said, 'Oh let not the Lord be angry, and I will speak again but this once. Suppose ten are found there.' He answered, 'For the sake of ten I will not destroy it'" (ESV, Gen 32:18).

Regrettably, in this story, the cities did not contain even ten righteous people to warrant their salvation. Nevertheless, God spared Lot and Abraham from impending destruction. God spared the only two righteous men in the unrighteous city. Though Lot resided amidst the wicked, he remained separate from their sinful ways:

"And Abraham went early in the morning to the place where he had stood before the LORD. And he looked down toward Sodom and Gomorrah and toward all the land of the valley, and he looked and, behold, the smoke of the land went up like the smoke of a furnace.

"So it was that, when God destroyed the cities of the valley, God remembered Abraham and sent Lot out of the midst of the

overthrow when he overthrew the cities in which Lot had lived" (ESV, Gen 19:27-29).

No matter the tragedies around us, if we remain faithful to the Lord, we can find comfort in His ability to safeguard our lives, shield us from harm, and bestow blessings upon us, even amid chaos and devastation. Additionally, we can take comfort in knowing that, like Abraham, we possess the power to intercede through prayer, potentially averting disaster and calamity from our nation.

Personal Story: What Motivates You?

Two days ago, I asked my kids to tidy their bedrooms before dinner. I offered them the incentive of having ice cream for dessert if they completed the task. While my daughters diligently worked, I noticed my son was unfocused, occasionally tidying up but mostly lost in thought. Recognizing his lack of motivation, I informed him that if he didn't pick up the pace, he'd not only miss out on dessert but also lose his soccer trading cards for a week. My intention wasn't to punish him; rather, I was eager to enjoy ice cream with them after dinner. The threat emerged after multiple attempts to motivate him solely with the promise of a reward—I was seeking a response.

Unfortunately, some individuals aren't sufficiently motivated by the rewards and blessings promised by the Lord to those who follow His teachings promptly. We've all been there. We postpone seeking God until we're at our wit's end, having exhausted all other options due to our circumstances spiraling out of control. While the Lord doesn't inflict punishment upon us in the manner of the Old Testament, He may withhold blessings, akin to how I was willing to do with my son. This principle is echoed in Exodus 34:6-7 (NASB):

> "...The LORD, the LORD God, compassionate and merciful, slow to anger, and abounding in faithfulness and truth; who keeps faithfulness for thousands, who forgives wrongdoing, violation of His Law, and sin; yet He will by no means leave the guilty unpunished, inflicting the punishment of fathers on the children and on the grandchildren to the third and fourth generations."

He desires to bless and reward us far more than we yearn for blessings ourselves. Just like with Nineveh, God will go to great extents to see that we get back on track with Him. All we need to do is repent and turn from our sinful ways. He is ready to restore us and pour abundant blessings on our lives again.

Questions to Reflect

Have I ever gone through any hardships leading to my turning to the Lord?

_____

_____

_____

Do I see some of these same "signs" or trials happening in my Nation today?

_____

_____

_____

Am I willing to turn to the Lord wholeheartedly and bring a change to my family, my city, and my country?

_____

_____

_____

Breakthrough Prayer

Thank you, Lord, for being compassionate, slow to anger, and eager to show us grace. I pray today for my family, my church, my community, and my nation. Have mercy on us and give us another chance to turn from our wicked ways and live for you. Forgive us, wash us from our sin, and shed light on any areas in which we displease you. Use me as You used Abraham to intercede for those around me. Use me to bring about the change that is needed in this Nation. I am willing. In Jesus name. Amen.

Day Twenty-two

Two Groups of People That Needed God's Mercy

In the story of Jonah, we encounter two contrasting types of people seeking a second chance from God. First, there's Jonah, who had faithfully walked with the Lord in obedience. Then, he reached a point where he felt God's demands had exceeded his limits and blatantly chose to follow his path instead. Another group of people included the pagan sailors and the Ninevites. Neither of them knew the Lord to begin with. They worshipped false gods and lived a life that did not please God. Unlike Jonah, they were not fully aware of their sin. Regardless of the start of their journey, both types of people were headed for destruction, whether they understood it or not. They both desperately needed a second chance from God.

Life Lesson # 22: God Doesn't Play Favorites

The two groups of people we described are defined in the gospels. It might seem like people like Jonah, who have been serving the Lord for a long time, would get extra "grace" for the good deeds they had previously performed. However, that is not what the Scriptures show us. "The Parable of the Prodigal Son" (Luke 15:11-32), "The Parable of the Laborers in the Vineyard" (Matthew 20), and "The

Parable of the Ten Virgins" (Matthew 25) demonstrate that is not how long ago we started our walk with the Lord that matters, but how we finish our race instead. Although there are rewards for those who are faithful, there is no preference for the one who knew the Lord sooner than the other. That attitude would create an uneven playing field in our walk with Christ, where the ones who get saved later in life would feel at a disadvantage.

I used to have that 'religious' attitude myself. I truly believed that because I had been walking with the Lord for longer than others, I deserved preferential treatment from the Lord, like an employee who had been working for a company for many years, as opposed to a brand-new worker. However, the Lord showed me that is not how He judges people. In fact, His rewards are 'performance-based' I know that doesn't seem very loving, but in fact, it is. It's the fairest type of treatment because it depends on us. The rewards we receive are in direct correlation with our choices. It's similar to a company whose employees' salary is based on their performance. The new employee can outperform the one who has been there for 20 years if they do what's right. This concept is exemplified in "The Parable of the Talents." God rewarded the one who multiplied the talents. He did not divide it equally, nor did He give more to the one that "needed it the most," or even justified the one who "had a good excuse." This same concept was illustrated in the parable of the laborers in the vineyards; He rewarded the laborers who came in last with the same pay as the ones that have been working all day. In John 15:1-8 (NASB) Jesus also illustrates this principle:

> *"I am the true vine, and My Father is the vinedresser. Every branch in Me that does not bear fruit, He takes away; and every branch that bears fruit, He prunes it so that it may bear more fruit. You are already clean because of the word which I have spoken to you. Remain in Me, and I in you. Just as the branch cannot bear fruit of itself but must remain in*

the vine, so neither can you unless you remain in Me. I am the vine, you are the branches; the one who remains in Me, and I in him bears much fruit, for apart from Me you can do nothing. If anyone does not remain in Me, he is thrown away like a branch and dries up; and they gather them and throw them into the fire, and they are burned. If you remain in Me, and My words remain in you, ask whatever you wish, and it will be done for you. My Father is glorified by this, that you bear much fruit, and so prove to be My disciples".

God looks at the fruit in a person's life as proof that they are true disciples. Otherwise, they are cut off and thrown into the fire. He does not count how long we have been going to church or any other superficial proof of our faith. He looks at where our faith is today.

Why are these parables important to understand in the light of Jonah's story? Because Jonah was not getting a 'free pass' based on his position as prophet of God, or based on his past performance (2 Kings 14:25), or based on his nationality as an Israelite. Jonah was headed for death and hell if it wasn't for the mercy of God, regardless of his tenure. Philippians 2:12-13 (NASB) warns us against growing complacent by saying:

"So then, my beloved, just as you have always obeyed, not as in my presence only, but now much more in my absence, work out your own salvation with fear and trembling; for it is God who is at work in you, both to desire and to work for His good pleasure".

That being said, it is never wise to take this concept and use it to live away from the Lord as long as possible because, like we are warned in Luke 12:20, what if today is our last day?

Jonah's reluctance to fully commit to God's assignment is a recurring theme in Christianity. Many individuals are comfortable with certain aspects of the Bible or specific ministry tasks, but when called upon to go further or deeper by God, they struggle to comply. Instead of moving forward, they may choose to retreat, evade, go through the motions, or pursue anything else except what God is asking of them, which only delays the inevitable, brings frustration, and might lead them away from God altogether.

God constantly works on our hearts until the day we leave this earth. He addresses different parts of who we are to shape us into reflections of Himself. His assignments intentionally target those 'sensitive' areas of our lives. They are not intended to purposefully make us uncomfortable but to bring healing, transformation, and improvement. When we resist His work in those areas, we are not only disobedient but also missing out on the breakthrough the Lord sought to give us through that journey.

Consider this scenario: someone faithfully attends church, tithes, serves, and loves their family. Yet, they stagnate spiritually because they refuse to venture beyond these predictable actions. Perhaps God prompts them to share their faith at work, but they dismiss it; maybe God urges them to forgive someone who deeply wounded them, yet they stubbornly cling to resentment. There might even be cases as significant as a pastor leading a congregation but hesitating to yield to any changes the Holy Spirit might want to bring because He's grown accustomed to doing things a certain way.

Personal Story: Pastor Opened Up to Change

Many years ago, during my teenage years in Argentina, a profound revival swept across the nation. At that time, I attended a traditional Baptist church, but as the revival reached our congregation, the youth eagerly embraced it first. Worship transformed from quiet to energetic, from dull to exciting, from reserved to a celebration. Teenagers filled the sanctuary, joyfully leaping, running, raising their hands, and dancing.

Our pastor, who had faithfully led the church for three decades, held deeply conservative views. While profoundly knowledgeable in Theology and Scripture, he had never encountered anything quite like this revival. I vividly recall one day when he addressed the congregation, assuring us that this movement was of the Lord and rooted in biblical principles. Though admitting his struggle to adapt to this new form of worship due to his upbringing, he declared his resolve not to hinder it and urged everyone to embrace it.

Initially, the youth embraced the revival far more readily than the older congregation members. However, The Holy Spirit permeated the entire church community over time, bridging generational differences.

Rebellion doesn't always manifest as an overt sin that everyone readily identifies. It can be as subtle as a seasoned believer who, unlike the pastor from my upbringing, resists allowing the Holy Spirit to work in his life simply because it doesn't align with his personal preferences. The Bible warns us that such rebellion "grieves the Holy Spirit" (Isaiah 63:10).

The apostle Paul admonishes us by stating:

"Do not grieve the Holy Spirit of God, by whom you were sealed for the day of redemption" (NASB, Ephesians 4:30).

As we deepen our relationship with the Lord, He calls us to press further into Him continually. Spiritual growth is ongoing; there's no final destination. The challenges the Lord presents to us may evolve, becoming more specific to our situation and refined compared to the initial stages of our journey. They might not always be as straightforward and obvious. People might not notice that we are taking steps closer to the Lord, and we might not get the recognition we once got as "new believers," but it's still worth pursuing because the Lord does notice and rewards us publicly for what we do in secret (Matthew 6:3-4).

In Psalm 139:23-24 (NASB), David wrote a prayer that we can adopt, asking God to reveal any areas of our lives that might go against His word:

> *"Search me, God, and know my heart;*
> *Put me to the test and know my anxious thoughts;*
> *And see if there is any hurtful way in me,*
> *And lead me in the everlasting way".*

You might find yourself in one of these two groups of people today. Perhaps, until now, you haven't delved much into understanding God, and consequently, your life hasn't reflected His love and freedom. Alternatively, your life may appear "ideal" from an external perspective. You might even hold a position within the Church where people admire you, yet you recognize that, at some point, your heart began to stray from God. You go through the motions, but your heart isn't fully invested in your actions. There's no passion; you've lost touch with your initial fervor. In 1 John 1:6-10 (NASB), it is stated:

> *"If we say that we have fellowship with Him and yet walk in the darkness, we lie and do not practice the truth; but if we walk in the Light as He Himself is in the Light, we have fellowship with one another, and the blood of Jesus His Son cleanses us from all sin. If we say that we have no sin, we are deceiving ourselves and the truth is not in us. If we confess our sins, He is faithful and righteous, so that He will forgive us our sins and cleanse us from all unrighteousness. If we say that we have not sinned, we make Him a liar and His word is not in us."*

Regardless of where you find yourself, God is capable of forgiving you, cleansing you from all sin, and renewing your life. You don't require a grand Church conference or the presence of a Pastor to reconcile with God. Some of the most profound encounters I've experienced with the Lord began at home, during my private prayer time. If you earnestly call upon Him, He will respond. Jeremiah 33:3 (NASB) declares: *"Call to Me, and I will answer you, and I will tell you great and mighty things, which you do not know."*

He doesn't expect a "perfect prayer" from us, nor does He demand that we "straighten up" before approaching Him. We can cry out to Him from the depths of despair, just like Jonah in the belly of the great fish, on our deathbeds, or like the criminal hanging next to Jesus on the cross. It's never too late to call out to God. He hears us and saves us right where we are.

Questions to Reflect

Which group of people do I identify myself with?

_____
_____
_____

Do I truly believe God is interested in my life and can do something about my situation?

_____
_____
_____

If I am not in one of those two groups, am I showing compassion and mercy towards those living away from God and needing His salvation today?

_____
_____
_____

Am I taking steps to share His love and forgiveness toward those in need?

_____
_____
_____

Breakthrough Prayer

Thank you, Lord, that You do not show favoritism. You are ready and willing to listen to my prayer no matter where I find myself. Please shed light on any area that might not align with your will and help me run to You with all my heart. I am willing to live for You wholeheartedly, no matter what You require of me. Thank You for your mercy and grace in my life. In Jesus' name. Amen.

Day Twenty-three

God Restored Nineveh (3:10-4:11)

"When God saw their deeds, that they turned from their evil way, then God relented of the disaster which He had declared He would bring on them. So He did not do it" (NASB, Jonah 3:10).

God withdrew His judgment towards Nineveh because He witnessed their heart transformation. The nation as a whole "turned from their evil ways." We tend to understand the concept of repentance as "a prayer where we ask God to forgive us for our sins." While prayer is undoubtedly a component of repentance, as seen in this instance alongside fasting, genuine repentance involves actions that demonstrate a sincere change. John the Baptist, for example, admonished the religious leaders to:

"Bring forth fruit that is consistent with repentance [let your lives prove your change of heart]" (AMP, Matthew 3:8).

Our actions evidence a genuinely repentant heart. Bearing this concept in mind, this would normally be a moment of celebration in someone's ministry. The sinners repented, and God extended mercy towards them. But this is not the case in this narrative. Jonah observed God's relenting from the judgment and got upset:

"But it greatly displeased Jonah, and he became angry. Then he prayed to the Lord and said, "Please Lord, was this not what I said when

I was still in my own country? Therefore in anticipation of this I fled to Tarshish, since I knew that You are a gracious and compassionate God, slow to anger and abundant in mercy, and One who relents of disaster. So now, Lord, please take my life from me, for death is better to me than life" (NASB, Jonah 4:1-3).

Why Was Jonah So Angry?

One of the reasons for Jonah's anger might have been his tarnished reputation. When a prophet's word did not come to fruition, they were considered a "false prophet." False prophets were not tolerated. Because God relented from bringing judgment to Nineveh, Jonah ran the risk of being perceived as a false prophet. Indeed, "Rabbinic literature suggests that based on Deuteronomy 18:21-22, he would be deemed a false prophet."[44] This fear likely fueled Jonah's discontentment towards God. However, the real reason that he didn't believe Nineveh deserved forgiveness was because "he believed that the Jews should experience divine mercy while the Gentiles should face divine judgment and punishment."[45] Jonah had obeyed God, traveled to Ninevah, and shared the warning with the number one enemy of his nation, Israel, but his heart was not in it. He still believed they needed to be punished and shown no mercy.

Life Lesson # 23:
Be Real with God

Upon initially looking into this part of the story, my automatic response leaned toward criticism of Jonah. How could he be so prideful and arrogant? He had been the recipient of divine grace and forgiveness himself. He had just been spared from death and hell from his disobedience and was now being judgmental towards others?! At first glance, it may seem justified to cast Jonah in such a bad light, and there is undoubtedly some truth to that, but there's another facet of this story that I want to highlight: the intimate relationship between Jonah and God.

Despite Jonah's apparent frustrations, he maintained a remarkable openness with God, expressing his genuine emotions without reservation. Jonah felt comfortable talking with God as one would confide in a trusted friend, unburdened by the fear of punishment. While his words may not have been disrespectful per se, they undeniably revealed the true sentiments residing within his heart. On the other hand, we see God speaking to Jonah similarly. He did not get offended by Jonah's feelings but engaged in the dialogue with him:

> "But the LORD said, "Do you have a good reason to be angry?"" (NASB, Jonah 4:4)

God rebuked Jonah, yes, but not out of a condemning heart, but out of love and genuine care for him. God's love is not weak. It's not an agreeable kind of love, either. God is strong, unwavering and He is not concerned about being "liked by us". Like a true Father, He loves us enough to bring correction for our good. Proverbs 3:11-12 (NASB) states:

> "My son, do not reject the discipline of the LORD
> Or loathe His rebuke,
> For whom the LORD loves He disciplines,
> Just as a father disciplines the son in whom he delights."

Jonah had experienced God's saving grace firsthand, yet he struggled to extend that same grace to the Assyrians. Such a lack of compassion was unacceptable to God and required addressing, but

Jonah was stubborn and pretty stuck in his ways, so God got creative, yet again, in order to communicate with Jonah more effectively:

> *"Then Jonah left the city and sat down east of it. There he made a shelter for himself and sat under it in the shade, until he could see what would happen in the city. So the* Lord *God designated a plant, and it grew up over Jonah to be a shade over his head, to relieve him of his discomfort. And Jonah was overjoyed about the plant. But God designated a worm when dawn came the next day, and it attacked the plant and it withered. And when the sun came up God designated a scorching east wind, and the sun beat down on Jonah's head so that he became faint, and he begged with all his soul to die, saying, "Death is better to me than life!"* (NASB, Jonah 4:5-8).

God communicated with Jonah in the manner most effective for him: through actions. Prior to this, God had demonstrated the importance of obedience, grace, and compassion through the storm and the great fish sent to rescue him. Now, God employed yet another tangible example—a "real-life analogy"—to underscore His care for Nineveh, employing the plant and the worm to convey His message to Jonah:

> *"But God said to Jonah, "Do you have a good reason to be angry about the plant?" And he said, "I have good reason to be angry, even to the point of death!"* (Jonah 4:9).

God asked him the same question one more time. And Jonah still responded in anger, this time even desiring his own death over this issue.

Personal Story: Learning to be Authentic

Growing up, I was pretty shy and rarely shared my true feelings. I just wanted people to like me. I also did not want to inconvenience anyone around me, so I would either not say anything or say something that sounded like the "right thing to say." When I got married, I soon realized this aspect of my personality would not work because my husband could not 'read my mind'! Whenever we had to decide on something, I struggled to express my honest feelings. I would always say, "Whatever you decide is fine." I was not necessarily being dishonest about my feelings, but I had difficulty narrowing down what I wanted. Also, I was afraid that he would not like my decision. I remember dropping hints, but I was never straightforward, and then I would get frustrated when he wouldn't pick what I was hoping for. Eventually, I had to learn to be direct and bold about who I was, what I wanted, and what I was all about. I am so thankful to God for this because it led me to develop into a more confident person who is real and more straightforward with others.

In our relationship with God, He expects us to be authentic and express ourselves freely to Him, just like we would with a spouse or a best friend. Yes, He already knows us and He can actually read our minds, but He still expects us to communicate like we would with a friend. That's how we develop that intimate friendship with Him. He truly cares, He will not get offended by our true feelings, and He will respond positively, even when what we think or want does not sound so 'proper.' We cannot be lazy in this area. Just like I had to work on communicating with my husband, we all need to make an effort in our relationship with God and be honest and raw about what we really want; the more we open up, the more natural it becomes. He is eager and willing to hear from us, and unlike others around us, He is never too busy for us!

Jonah was not proper or nice about his feelings, in fact, he was clearly wrong, but God did not abandon him or retaliate for these feelings. He engaged in the dialogue. Sometimes we tend to mask our emotions with spiritual-sounding phrases. We say one thing, while we really mean something else and wonder why our results are not reflecting our hearts. This behavior is born out of a fear and it will hinder us in every area of our lives: in business, marriage, or our relationship with God. 1 John 4:18 (NASB) states:

> *"There is no fear in love, but perfect love drives out fear, because fear [a] involves punishment, and the one who fears is not perfected in love."*

Authenticity with God is the catalyst for a breakthrough. It demands honesty with ourselves and the courage to articulate our genuine feelings without fearing repercussions. Unlike an abusive or passive-aggressive figure, God is a safe, trustworthy and compassionate Father who welcomes our raw emotions. The most impactful prayers aren't the polished ones but rather those that emanate from the depths of our hearts. Hebrews 4:15-16 (NASB) states:

> *"For we do not have a high priest who cannot sympathize with our weaknesses, but One who has been tempted in all things just as we are, yet without sin. Therefore let's approach the throne of grace with confidence, so that we may receive mercy and find grace for help at the time of our need."*

Jesus went through every human emotion and struggle, and He can sympathize with us. God wants us to come boldly to him, to be real. He will not reject us. Jonah was the perfect example of this. He was completely "improper," first in his actions, then in his speech, but the Lord did not reject him. He did not condone his behavior either, in fact, God spoke the truth to Jonah.

As Proverbs 27:5-6 (NASB) wisely states,

*"Better is open rebuke
Than love that is concealed.
Faithful are the wounds of a friend,
But deceitful are the kisses of an enemy."*

Proverbs 28:23 states:

*"One who rebukes a person will afterward find more favor
Than one who flatters with the tongue."*

Firm guidance and honest communication are necessary in order to break free from self-destructive patterns and embrace truth. Let's be brave enough not only to be open about our feelings to God but also to be open to everything that God wants to say to us, knowing that his intentions for us are always for our good. Sometimes, what God communicates may not align with our desires, yet it's precisely what we need to hear to get out of our desperate situation and onto our breakthrough.

Questions to Reflect

Do I feel at ease talking to God?

Do I believe He genuinely likes me and is interested in who I am, and my real raw feelings, desires, and even questions?

Do I think God can get offended by my honesty? Do I believe He is a "safe person" in my life, with whom I can be completely honest without holding back?

Breakthrough Prayer

Dear God, help me to develop a genuine and truthful relationship with you, where I can be open about my true feelings, thoughts, concerns, and even questions. Help me to be open to what You have to say to me as well, knowing that even if it's not what I want to hear, it's always for my good, because your heart for me is always to bless me and set me free from things that are holding me back. Thank You that I can trust You with who I am. In Jesus' name. Amen.

Day Twenty-four

The Root of Jonah's Frustration

Jonah's reaction to the death of a plant that offered him temporary shade raises a poignant contrast: he displayed anger over the loss of personal comfort yet seemed indifferent to the fate of an entire nation. His assertion of having "the right to be angry" underscores his boldness and conviction in his emotions, suggesting a skewed sense of priorities. This begs the question: what sort of prophet, tasked with conveying God's message, exhibits such self-centeredness and disregard for the well-being of others?

Life Lesson # 24:
That Thing That Aggravates You is There by Design

The answer lies in that he was just like you and me. God often selects and empowers imperfect individuals for significant tasks. Have you ever wondered why God singled out Jonah for such a pivotal assignment instead of choosing a different prophet without profound reservations about the Assyrians? It might seem more straightforward. However, the explanation likely is that Jonah's mission was intricately tied to his personal growth. God intended to address Jonah's character flaws through this assignment. Jonah needed to cultivate compassion and extend love beyond his familiar boundaries, and this journey was precisely how God guided him toward that transformation.

Many times, in our lives, God calls us to do the very opposite of what our flesh desires. He calls us to assignments that may seem incredible to someone else but are not necessarily within our comfort zone or area of expertise at first glance. Why does He do that? Because God is not only interested in using us to bless others; He is also looking to perfect us in the process.

Have you ever felt frustrated in your calling, thinking that someone else might have done this job a lot better or easier? That's the key. We are not meant to perform His work within our own abilities; we need Him to work in us the desire to do it, the provision, the strength, and even the heart toward the people we are to minister to.

Paul, once a persecutor of Christians, was called by God to become a preacher for Christ. What sense does this make in the natural? It's precisely in these instances, when such a transformation defies human logic, that we can tell that it is in fact a true calling from God.

Personal Story: God Dealt with My Pride Through This Assignment

When the Lord called me to leave my career and stay home to raise my children, it was not easy. Let's just say it was different from what I had envisioned for my life. I was certainly grateful for the opportunity, but it was challenging to say the least.

I remember how much it would affect me when people would ask what I did for a living, or the many remarks I would get about it. I was just doing it to be obedient to God, but my motives were being questioned. I was put down because of my choice to be a "homemaker." It humbled me deeply, but it taught me to not pay attention to other people's opinions about me, only God's! It took many years to get there, but it was so worthy. I was able to surrender my ego and just allow God to lead my life.

I didn't know where this journey would lead, but I followed God one step at a time and trusted His timing. Almost 9 years later, the Lord is giving me new dreams, a lot better and more purposeful than the career I left behind when He called me to raise my kids! The best part of it is that He dealt with heart, to prepare me for the criticism I would encounter in the next stage in life. Today I can say that criticism is not fun, but it doesn't affect me nearly as much as it did back them, because I have come to know how much I mean to God. His plans are trustworthy and so much better than any human being could ever come up with!

His plans are trustworthy and so much better than any human being could ever come up with!

Just as He cherished Jonah and the Ninevites, His love extends to you and me. He has magnificent plans for our lives, even when circumstances suggest otherwise.

Jonah was indeed a prophet of God; his status was recognized through recorded events where his delivered message came to fruition. Yet, even with his prophetic calling, aspects of his character required refinement. It's a reminder that regardless of the duration of one's walk with the Lord or involvement in ministry, we are not immune to God's ongoing work within our hearts. He tirelessly shapes us to mirror the 'Image of Christ'. Romans 8:28-29 (NASB) serves as a testament to this:

> *"And we know that God causes all things to work together for good to those who love God, to those who are called according to His purpose. For those whom He foreknew, He also predestined to become conformed to*

the image of His Son, so that He would be the firstborn among many brothers and sisters."

Jonah seemed to be needing to be transformed into the likeness of Christ in areas like compassion, surrender, humility, and obedience. Who are we to pass judgment on him? We all harbor areas needing significant refinement; let's refrain from deceiving ourselves into believing we have it all figured out.

Jonah would never have recognized this truth had God not tasked him with an uncomfortable assignment. Similarly, I wouldn't have noticed these weaknesses in my character had I remained confined to my office job, distant from the challenges of raising children at home. Wherever God calls you during this season, recognize that it's not only about those you're called to serve but also about the transformation He's implementing within you, through that mission. Embrace it wholeheartedly and endure the test, so that you may develop into the person He designed you to be! It's worth it!

Questions to Reflect

What difficult situations or people am I facing right now?

_____

_____

_____

What is my overall attitude towards these hardships?

_____

_____

_____

Have I embraced them as part of God's purpose, or am I resisting them because they do not fit my ideal scenario?

_____

_____

_____

Breakthrough Prayer

Thank you, Lord, for having deep purposes for my life. Thank You for making me realize that even those challenging situations will be a tool to shape me into the person I am meant to become. Please help me embrace the hardships as part of your master plan, knowing that You are with me and will turn all those situations for my good. In Jesus' name. Amen.

Day Twenty-five

Ninevah Was Spared, But Not Forever

The city of Nineveh did indeed repent at the time of Jonah, and as a result, it was spared from immediate judgment. However, regrettably, its repentance was short-lived. It returned to its wicked ways, and "God's judgment eventually did fall on the city."[46]

This destruction occurred approximately 100 years after their initial repentance. This timespan typically represents the transition from one generation to the next. The generation that had witnessed Jonah's warning and experienced repentance had most likely passed away. Consequently, the subsequent generation either was unaware of or disregarded the lessons of their forebears. This disregard for the past led to dreadful consequences, culminating in "the king of the Assyrians leading his army to destroy the northern kingdom of Israel and oppress even Judah for a time" (2 Kings 17:6, 18:13-14).

The account of the destruction of Nineveh can be found in the book of Nahum. Displeased with Nineveh's actions, God dispatched another prophet, Nahum, to prophesy the city's downfall. Additionally, the prophet Zephaniah delivered a message of judgment against them (Zephaniah 2:13). God had patience and grace towards the people of Nineveh, but they would not listen. These series of warnings culminated in the city's destruction in 612 BC.[47]

Jonah Was a Picture of Jesus

The book of Jonah is "one of the most cited Old Testament books by the church fathers."[48] As a matter of fact, Jesus Himself made reference to Jonah during His ministry (Matthew 12:41; Luke 11:32). Furthermore, Jesus predicted His death and resurrection three days later by likening it to the time Jonah spent in the belly of the fish.[49] According to Matthew 12:38-41(NASB), the Pharisees and teachers of the law said to Jesus:

> *"Then some of the scribes and Pharisees said to Him, "Teacher, we want to see a sign from You." But He answered and said to them, "An evil and adulterous generation craves a sign; and so no sign will be given to it except the sign of Jonah the prophet; for just as JONAH WAS IN THE STOMACH OF THE SEA MONSTER FOR THREE DAYS AND THREE NIGHTS, so will the Son of Man be in the heart of the earth for three days and three nights. The men of Nineveh will stand up with this generation at the judgment, and will condemn it because they repented at the preaching of Jonah; and behold, something greater than Jonah is here."*

In Luke 11:29-30 (NASB) we read the following:

> *"Now as the crowds were increasing, He began to say, "This generation is a wicked generation; it demands a sign, and so no sign will be given to it except the sign of Jonah. For just as Jonah became a sign to the Ninevites, so will the Son of Man be to this generation."*

Jesus used the conversion of the Ninevites, who were non-Jews, "as a means to chastise the Jews who were rejecting His message."[49] This comparison elucidates how Jesus came to fulfill and transcend the Old Covenant and inaugurate the New Covenant, now entrusted to the Gentiles[50]. This parallel with the story of Jonah was also intended to facilitate the Jewish people's understanding that the

God of the Old Testament is the same God who sent Jesus[51]. He had demonstrated care for other nations in the Old Testament and now, through Jesus, was extending the opportunity for salvation to every nation. The book of Jonah serves as a "foreshadowing of the Gentiles coming to faith in the one true God." [52]

There are numerous parallels between Jonah and Jesus, highlighted even by Jesus himself through illustrations. However, this doesn't imply an absolute comparison between the two. In fact, they diverge significantly in several aspects. While Jonah resisted obedience, Jesus embraced it willingly. Jonah harbored contempt for the Ninevites, whereas Jesus demonstrated love for sinners. Jonah's reluctance led him to avoid delivering his message even at the cost of his life, whereas Jesus willingly sacrificed himself to offer salvation. While they are not equals in any sense, Jonah's narrative serves as a foreshadowing of God's plan of salvation and His outreach to the gentiles.

Jonah's three days inside the fish foreshadowed Jesus' three days in the tomb preceding His resurrection: "The book of Jonah stands as an important link in the prophetic chain, giving readers a glimpse of Christ's death and resurrection hundreds of years before they actually occurred."[53]

Life Lesson # 25:
Love for "Outsiders" and Forgiveness

The book of Jonah vividly illustrates God's compassion for those traditionally regarded as "outsiders." In the Old Testament, these outsiders are often called 'pagan nations'. This sentiment extended into Jesus's ministry, where He summoned His disciples to preach to Jews and Gentiles alike. Furthermore, Jesus emphasized including the marginalized. In His day, He engaged with people who were deemed less important, like women, tax collectors, sinners, lepers, and foreigners. Mark 2:15-17 (NASB) captures this ethos:

> *"And it happened that He was reclining at the table in his house, and many tax collectors and sinners were dining with Jesus and His disciples; for there were many of them, and they were following Him. When the scribes of the Pharisees saw that He was eating with the sinners and tax collectors, they said to His disciples, "Why is He eating with tax collectors and sinners?" And hearing this, Jesus said to them, "It is not those who are healthy who need a physician, but those who are sick; I did not come to call the righteous, but sinners."*

Jonah's book illustrates God's heart for all people, including the worst of sinners.

The Lord desires us to extend that same compassion and grace He gave us to others. We are often happy to receive the grace that God gifts us, but when it comes time for us to be gracious to others, we are not always as willing to do so.

Matthew 5:43-48 (NASB) Jesus said:

> *"You have heard that it was said, 'You shall love your neighbor and hate your enemy.' But I say to you, love your enemies and pray for those who persecute you, so that you may prove yourselves to be sons of your Father who is in heaven; for He causes His sun to rise on the evil and the good, and sends rain on the righteous and the unrighteous. For if you love those who love you, what reward do you have? Even the tax collectors, do they not do the same? And if you greet only your brothers and sisters, what more are you doing than others? Even the Gentiles, do they not do the same? Therefore you shall be perfect, as your heavenly Father is perfect."*

Jesus also admonished us to forgive one another so that God may forgive us in turn:

"For if you forgive other people for their offenses, your heavenly Father will also forgive you. But if you do not forgive other people, then your Father will not forgive your offenses" (NASB, Matthew 6:14-15).

Forgiveness is part of the requirement for God to forgive us. We are granted the unmerited privilege of being forgiven, but we are expected to forgive others in return. In the book of Matthew, we can see the "Parable of the Unforgiving Servant," where the servant who was forgiven a huge debt by his master was not willing to forgive a small debt to his servant. As a result, Jesus concluded the story by saying that:

> **We are granted the unmerited privilege of being forgiven, but we are expected to forgive others in return.**

"Then summoning him, his master said to him, 'You wicked slave, I forgave you all that debt because you pleaded with me. Should you not also have had mercy on your fellow slave, in the same way that I had mercy on you?' And his master, moved with anger, handed him over to the torturers until he would repay all that was owed him. My heavenly Father will also do the same to you, if each of you does not forgive his brother from your heart" (NASB, Matthew 18:32-35).

Let's extend forgiveness to those who have wronged us and offer the kind of love Christ offered us to all people, regardless of who they are or what they have done.

Questions to Reflect

Who do I choose to forgive and release into God's hands today?

_____

_____

_____

Is it difficult for me to receive and accept God's forgiveness for myself?

_____

_____

_____

Am I able to forgive myself and see myself as God sees me?

_____

_____

_____

Breakthrough Prayer

Dear God, Thank You for your forgiveness. Today, I forgive those who have wronged me, my family, or even my Nation. I surrender into your hands the pain and suffering they have caused me and I choose to offer them the same grace You have freely offered me. Take away any root of bitterness, resentment, pride or unforgiveness that may still be in my heart and set me free to love those whom You have died for.

Help me to see people with Your eyes and reflect Your heart for humankind. Please forgive me of all my sin today. I believe that You are my defender, and as I make the decision to forgive, You will, in return, forgive me and will turn all the wrongs into rights. Thank You for Your love, forgiveness, and Your freedom. In Jesus' name. Amen.

Day Twenty-six

Main Takeaways from the Life of Jonah

From the book of Jonah, we can derive numerous life lessons. At the beginning of the story, we learned about Israel's history of sin, rebellion, and repentance and how they became prideful as soon as God restored and blessed them. We learned about the consequences of disobedience and how we are to follow God's standards above our culture. We observed one more time how God is not offended when we are honest and raw with Him, He prefers that. We learned that God makes a way for us when we humble ourselves and ask for help and forgiveness. We learned about following His leading while at the same time doing our part.

We also looked into Jonah's reason for his rebellion and anger over Nineveh's repentance. Although there's a lot to be learned about Jonah's complex emotions and actions toward God and the Ninevites, the central focus of this book isn't Jonah himself; it's God.

The main narrative underscores God's boundless mercy, unfaltering patience, and readiness to heed the pleas of His people, even when they seem undeserving. God will forgive us when we wholeheartedly repent and cry out to Him. Just as He saved Jonah as an individual, He is also willing to extend His forgiveness to entire nations, as demonstrated in the case of Nineveh.

He is a God of justice who does not overlook our sin; however, He is always seeking ways to lead us to repentance and turn to Him, enabling us to receive His forgiveness and partake in His blessings.

He is a just God and does not overlook sin. Jonah faced severe consequences for his rebellion, and Nineveh stood on the brink of destruction due to their evil deeds and prideful attitude. However, God heard their cries and granted them a second chance. He looked beyond nationality and the color of their skin, disregarding the magnitude or duration of their sins. There was no favoritism towards Jonah for his past obedience, nor was Nineveh given less opportunity to repent due to the severity of their transgressions. God is impartial, offering everyone the chance to turn towards Him and receive His love, mercy, and forgiveness, irrespective of their circumstances.

God demonstrated patience with Jonah, persistently attempting various methods to help him comprehend His will. Similarly, He showed patience with the city of Nineveh, sending a prophet to warn them of their sins' repercussions. He is a God who actively communicates with His people, speaking through the words of the Bible, the wonders of nature, the circumstances of life, and the guidance of Pastors and Teachers. Even now, He is reaching out to you. Will you listen to His voice today and earnestly call upon Him from the depths of your heart?

Questions to Consider

Which life lessons from the book of Jonah resonated with me the most?

_____

_____

_____

Am I willing to accept God's mercy and forgiveness for myself today?

_____

_____

_____

Am I willing to extend the same mercy and grace towards others and be happy for them when God restores and blesses them?

_____

_____

_____

My Prayer over you

Thank you, Lord, for those who have joined me and persevered through this Journey. I pray that you bless them with insight and wisdom, as well as a desire to grow closer to you each day. Give them the victory to complete this last section of the 40-days, and open their spiritual eyes to see what is that you want them to. Bless them abundantly in every area of their lives. I pray that they not only get their needs met, but that you will grant them the desires of their hearts and mold their hearts to desire to go deeper in you above everything else. Remove any hindrance and bless them so that they can fulfill your purposes in their lives. In Jesus 'name. Amen.

Chapter 3:

Ruth: From Outcast to Royalty

Days 27 - 40

Day Twenty-seven

INTRODUCTION (RUTH 1:1)

The book of Ruth takes place in Bethlehem in Judah, located six miles south of Jerusalem, during "the days when the Judges ruled."[1] This was the place where Jesus was born."[2] It occurred between the death of Joshua and the rise of Samuel's influence (between 1150 and 1100 B.C), after Israel's conquest of Cannan, and before the rise of the monarchy.[3] This period parallels the time of Hannah. Bethlehem was only 11 miles from Ramah, where Hannah lived. Therefore, the same political, social, and spiritual chaos we discussed in Hannah's life applies to this narrative. It was a time of "lawlessness and chaos in Israel."[4] As we pointed out earlier, the book of Judges describes exactly how their society functioned: *"In those days there was no king in Israel. Everyone did what was right in his own eyes"* (ESV, Judges 21:25).

To add to these complex circumstances, Bethlehem was undergoing a famine. The book begins with the story of a family from Bethlehem, and it narrates their journey during this desperate time in their region:

> *"In the days when the judges ruled, there was a famine in the land. So a man from Bethlehem in Judah, together with his wife and two sons, went to live for a while in the country of Moab"* (ESV, Ruth 1:1).

Background on Famines

Before we delve deeper into their story, let me describe the background of a famine in those days. The word famine refers to "an acute and prolonged food shortage." In ancient times in Israel and Egypt, famines happened pretty frequently. Pandemics often came afterward due to the famine. According to a study conducted after the 2019 World Pandemic, "Both over- and undernutrition increase the severity of disease… further driving the disease and famine vicious cycle."[5] This is most likely what happened in ancient Israel. The food shortage turned into disease, which only made the crisis worse. The loss of life and suffering during a time like this was great.

According to the Scriptures, famines were the direct result of disobedience. The Bible usually mentions famines as a sign of "God's judgment."[6] Judging from the historical and political atmosphere, this particular famine was the direct result of Israel's noncompliance to God's commands.[7]

God had made a covenant with Israel. As long as they obeyed this covenant, they did not have to fear the famine because God had promised to provide for them (Deuteronomy 11:13–17). To be preserved in times of famine was a unique mark of God's favor and power (Job 5:20; Ps. 33:19; 37:19). The rain was in fact a reward from the Lord, if the people followed Him:

> "The LORD will open the heavens, the storehouse of his bounty, to send rain on your land in season and to bless all the work of your hands. You will lend to many nations but will borrow from none" (ESV, Deuteronomy 28:12).

God proved His faithfulness in this area when He sent a warning dream to Pharaoh about an upcoming famine, and then He gave Joseph both the interpretation and a strategy to prepare for it. As they followed God's plan, they became a blessing amid a famine, not only to their nation but also to other nations and Joseph's entire family (Gen 41). To clarify, not all famines were considered a punishment; some were simply a way for the Lord to lead His people to a new land.[8] However, in this context of Israel's long chain of disobedience, it is clear that their idolatry was what "had brought this judgment in the form of hunger and famine."[9]

ELIMELECH'S DESPERATE MOMENT (RUTH 1:2)

The family in this story was composed of Elimelech, his wife Naomi, and their two sons Mahlon and Chilion, who decided to leave the land the Lord had brought them into and go to Moab in light of their distress:

> *"The name of the man was Elimelech. and the name of his wife Naomi, and the names of his two sons were Mahlon and Chilion. They were Ephrathites from Bethlehem in Judah. They went into the country of Moab and remained there" (ESV, Ruth 1:2).*

It must have been a severe famine because Elimelech was a landowner in Bethlehem, and he had decided to leave everything behind.[10] It must have been a hard crisis for someone from Bethlehem to decide to go to Moab.

Moab had a bad reputation for several reasons. First, it was just not a "desirable area." Second, the Moabites were considered enemies of Israel (1 Samuel 12:9, 14:47).

Moving to Moab was not only an illogical idea, but it went against God's plans. Israel had already made that same mistake in the past and had paid a high price for it. When they rebelled against the Lord, they had decided to serve the gods of Moab, which resulted in eighteen years of oppression. This continued until they finally repented, put away the idols and the Lord delivered them" (Judges 10:6-18).[11] This very example should have served as a warning for Elimelech not to go there and expect blessings. The Lord had given His people the land of Bethlehem, which meant "house of bread," and as long as they kept the covenant, they could trust His provision. Moving to a foreign land without the blessing of the Lord was a recipe for disaster.

Elimelech was a Fool

Bethlehem, in Hebrew, means "House of Bread." Elimelech deliberately decided to leave the land where God had promised to bless them and go to a pagan nation in search of provision.[12] God had explicitly forbidden them from going to Moab. In addition to this, not long before that, the King of Moab had recruited a prophet to curse Israel and had schemed to have the Moabite women seduce the men of Israel to lead them to idolatry (Numbers 25).[13] Moving to Moab went against all sound judgment and clearly against God's will.

Elimelech, in the Hebrew language, means "God is King." His name is an indication that his parents were in covenant with God. The Israelites who followed God would have shared some of the stories of God's power to deliver Israel with their children. Elimelech, however, in the light of this famine, decided to find the solution on his own, away from God. He went to a neighboring nation that did not worship the God of Israel. He was searching for the solution to his problems away from the Lord.[14] Proverbs 14:12 (ESV) states: *"There is a way that appears to be right, but in the end it leads to death."*

It took them several days on foot to get from Bethlehem to Moab, which indicates that this was not meant as a "temporary move." It was not a decision that could have been reversed easily.[15]

Life Lesson # 27:
The Danger of Making Rash Decisions

Have you ever gone to the grocery store when you were hungry? If you are like me, when you are hungry, you tend to buy more than what you need and most likely make some bad choices. You are so hungry that you are not thinking clearly. How about when the COVID lockdowns in 2020 were announced? Didn't most people flock to the grocery stores and empty the shelves out of desperation? One of the items most coveted was toilet paper rolls…that did not make much sense, but people were frantic and were not necessarily thinking clearly. These may seem like fun anecdotes for those of us who lived through it and survived, but what happens in a real emergency? When our livelihoods are on the line? What if we were facing the tragedy that Elimelech and his family faced? Political turmoil, economic crisis, social chaos, and famine all wrapped up. What would our reaction be? Would we go into panic mode and follow what others are doing? Are we walking in wisdom and obedience to the Lord in times of peace so we are not caught off guard in times of turmoil?

People facing desperate situations can make drastic decisions, some of which can become irreversible. Proverbs 19:2 (AMP) states:

> *"Also, it is not good for a person to be without knowledge, and he who hurries with his feet [acting impulsively and proceeding without caution or analyzing the consequences] sins (misses the mark)."*

Although Israel was undergoing "the darkest of the dark days" in Israel, Elimelech did not seek God during his Desperate Moment. In contrast to Hannah and Jonah, He made a hasty decision to leave God. This drastic, rash decision affected not only himself but his entire family.

But how do we avoid making those mistakes? A famous quote states, "In times of peace, prepare for war." This concept is just as true in the natural as much as in the spiritual realm. Being grounded spiritually when things are going well will keep us from frantically panicking during the chaos. So, how do we prepare for those hard times so we don't act impulsively? One of the answers is to develop the habit of seeking God for His will in advance; He can give us insight into our future and directions that will help create a better tomorrow and prepare for unforeseen danger. Get used to listening to His voice in small everyday situations so that when the more significant choices arise, your ear is trained to hear His voice.

Years ago, in youth group, some students asked the pastor how to hear from God about the person you are meant to marry. This is a life-altering major decision, and you don't want to make a mistake in this area. Although this is a complex question, and the answer can vary depending on the specific scenario, I remember having the thought that 'the answer lies in first developing that sensitivity to God's voice for every other area of your life.' Once you learn how to hear His voice and follow Him in everyday decisions, when it comes time for life-changing decisions (like marriage or what to do during times of war, famine, or a pandemic), you can draw from that same ability to hear God and walk confidently knowing He is the one leading you.

If you live a life away from God, making decisions based on your preferences and plans regularly, hearing His voice regarding the big issues in life will be more challenging and the risk of missing it will be greater. If you are not in the habit of praying regularly and hearing the voice of God, what makes you think that when you are at a crossroads, you will be able to discern His voice from all the wrong voices out there? The enemy is an expert in disguising himself as "an angel of light" and imitating God's voice. We have to train our ears to discern the difference! Practice hearing His voice in the everyday mundane issues, and you will have a level of confidence about the future that nothing or no one can take from you.

Even when something seems like a great idea or a perfect solution, we must seek the Lord and His wisdom to ensure that we are making the right decision, that the timing is correct, and that our hearts are in the right place. No matter how old or long we've been walking with the Lord, we still need to seek Him for everything.

Personal Story: Follow Peace

I briefly shared part of this story on Day 20, but I wanted to provide a little more detail for the sake of this point. When I was in my late 20s, I moved to Florida after finishing Graduate School, and I was blessed to get a job in a small business that provided me with a work visa. Getting a job with a work visa is very hard, so this was huge for me!

While working there, I was also involved in my Church and doing a one-year Bible institute, and I had recently started dating my now husband. I was finally enjoying my life after many years of studying, moving, and uncertainty. Unfortunately, after working in that job for about a year, I was let go due to budget cuts. The tricky side was that if I did not find a new job willing to sponsor my work visa within a few weeks, I would be "out of status" and would have to move back to Argentina. I did not understand why God would allow that to happen. The timing could not have been more inconvenient!

I then applied to countless jobs and went to many interviews, but as I mentioned earlier, getting a job with a work visa was not easy. When my now husband realized, I would likely have to move to Argentina, he proposed to me. He knew he wanted to marry me eventually, so why not do that right away and solve the visa situation, right? As much as this seemed like a great solution, I was unsure. We had only known each other for four months, and I did not want to make a rash decision. It's a long story, but after going back and forth, praying a lot, and not knowing for sure, I decided to move back to Argentina. The truth is that I did not have complete clarity about what God was doing, but one thing I knew was that marriage is not a revocable decision.

There is more to the story, but the one thing I remember thinking is that I needed to follow "peace." I did not want to decide if I did not have complete peace about it. No circumstance is desperate enough to rush me into something.

I also remember assessing the circumstances all around me. All the doors were being closed. Everything I attempted would fall through. I understood this to indicate that God was closing those doors for a reason.

Finally, one day, as I was praying, the Lord gave me a Scripture confirming that I was to return to my home country. It was not an easy decision, but as soon as I made it, I had complete peace, and every step I took felt right again! I discovered that the Peace of God (Philippians 4:7) is worth far more than anything this world offers!

Moving back meant leaving everything behind with the possibility of never being back. I had to start over in Argentina after building my life in the States for the previous ten years; it was not going to be easy. All I had was a few hundred dollars, no car, no cell phone, and debt. It was humbling, but I knew the Lord was with me. I was at my lowest point, but I was finally at peace. Psalm 119:165 (NASB) states:

> *"Those who love Your Law have great peace,*
> *And nothing causes them to stumble."*

When we surrender our paths to the Lord, our decisions will not be made out of fear or survival but in faith. They might not make sense to others, but we will have His peace in the darkest hour, which will be enough to sustain us. The Lord did a wonderful work in my heart during my time in Argentina, and he ended up opening doors for me to come back to the United States, less than a year later, get married, and follow His will for my life. The Lord gave me this verse in Isaiah 31:1 (ESV) when I arrived in Argentina, and it says:

> *"Woe to those who go down to Egypt for help,*
> *who rely on horses,*
> *who trust in the multitude of their chariots*
> *and in the great strength of their horsemen,*
> *but do not look to the Holy One of Israel,*
> *or seek help from the L*ORD.*"*

I did not know if I would ever return to the United States again, but it did not matter because I knew the Lord was with me; if He had brought me to the U.S. in the first place, He could always open the doors for me to go back, if that were the best for me. He is my provider, not the economy of a country. His presence brings me joy, not the external aspects of my life. There is value in holding on to God consistently. We don't know when the hardships will come, but when they do, if we are with Him, we have nothing to fear. Don't make a life-altering decision based on fear. Desperation is not a legitimate reason to make a rash choice. Take the time to seek the Lord, and follow His peace even when it doesn't make sense.

Questions to Reflect

Have I taken the time to seek the Lord for significant life decisions?

___

Have I gotten into the habit of seeking His guidance for everyday affairs?

___

Am I willing to develop spiritual sensitivity to His voice so that I will always discern His perfect will for me?

___

What specific decisions do I need guidance on today?

Breakthrough Prayer

Lord, please help me to develop the habit of seeking You and getting in your Word in times of peace. Help me to create the "spiritual muscles" before the hardships arise so that I will be prepared for any and every battle ahead. Teach me how to hear Your voice and be obedient to Your leading in the most minor details of life so that I can also hear Your voice in the life-altering moments. Thank You for being right here with me. I love You. In Jesus' name. Amen.

Day Twenty-eight

Stepping Out of God's Will

Going to a far country, away from the land the Lord had given them, meant breaking the Law of Moses and getting out of "fellowship with God." This is the equivalent of us stepping outside of God's will when things get tough. Instead of staying where He called us to stay, whether in a marriage, a ministry, or an assignment, we sometimes seek a way out when things don't go how we expected them to.

I hear some people, after making wrong choices, say things like "God knows my heart" or "He understands my weaknesses." Unfortunately, good intentions don't make up for bad judgment. In the case of Elimelech, his rushed decision led to death: *"But Elimelech, the husband of Naomi, died, and she was left with her two sons"* (ESV, Ruth 1:.3).

Right away after they moved to Moab, Elimelech died, and his wife Naomi and her two sons were left alone in a foreign land without a father or a husband, which would be difficult today. In those days, it was a significant tragedy. He might have died of starvation, or maybe from sickness; we do not know the details, but what we know is that God did not cause that to happen; it was merely the consequence of his poor decision.

More Wrong Choices

Technically, Naomi could have returned to Bethlehem and sought help from their family members. She might have been young enough to marry one of the relatives, which is what the Israeli law allowed to protect young widows. But that's not what they did. Instead, Naomi and her two sons decided to stay in Moab and continued trying to fix their problems on their own, away from God:

> *"These took Moabite wives; the name of the one was Orpah and the name of the other Ruth. They lived there about ten years, and both Mahlon and Chilion died, so that the woman was left without her two sons and her husband"* (ESV, 1:4-5).

They stayed there for 10 years, they married Moabite women, which was in direct violation of God's laws, and they ended up suffering the same fate as their father, Elimelech.

The Lord had strictly forbidden the Israelites to intermarry with other nations because this could lead them to the sin of idolatry[15] (Deuteronomy 7:3-4). It was considered infidelity to the Lord"[16] and a violation of Israeli law[17]. This was not only sin, but it was also ridiculous, as "the Moabites were one of the most mistrusted and despised enemies of Israel. They were descendants of Lot's sexual relationship with his older daughter, and the Israelites had sexual relations with Moabite women in a cultic festival during the wilderness wanderings" (Numbers 25). The book of Deuteronomy says, "No. . . Moabite or any of their descendants may enter the assembly of the LORD, not even in the tenth generation" (Deuteronomy 23:3).[18] Sometimes God's commands seem harsh and even nonsensical, but as we obey Him, we will understand that they are meant for our protection, for our good, and that of our families in the future.

Elimelech made a choice when he decided to move his entire family to a foreign land, away from God's will. My first instinct was to justify Elimelech. Because of the famine, he "had to" move to provide for his family, but as I looked into this story further, I realized that this was a well-thought-out decision. They had to leave relatives and even land that he owned behind, bring a limited number of belongings, and walk for days to a land that, for starters, was not promising at all. At the end of the story, we will find out that many of their relatives and fellow Israelites stayed and survived. God cared for them in their land; moving away was unnecessary.

Elimelech followed his way of doing things and thus modeled this type of behavior to his children. After their father died, they chose to stay in Moab and commit the sin of "intermarriage," which did not end up well. They were married for about ten years, but none had any children, which was another massive misfortune in those days. After those ten years, Mahlon and Chilion died, and just like their father, they left two widows behind, alongside their widowed mother.

Life Lesson # 28:
Consulting the Lord Before Every Decision

Personal Story: Choosing the Right School

When my oldest son was about to enter Kindergarten, I wanted to ensure we chose the right school. We toured most schools in the area but did not have peace about any of them. One day my husband mentioned someone we knew had told him about a homeschooling co-op they were a part of. This was not part of our plan and had never even crossed my mind, but because I felt like none of the other choices felt right, I decided to do a tour and give it a chance. When I pray about a decision, I always remain open to every possibility. I try not to rule out any options unless the Lord closes that door, because I've seen God lead me before, and He is not always as predictable as some may picture Him as. In fact, He loves to surprise us with new and innovative ways of solving our dilemmas. We just have to be open.

I remember going to the orientation meeting with my husband and against all odds, we both had peace about it. The fact that even my husband agreed to this, seemed like the biggest confirmation to me. We then decided to sign up, and little did we know that a few months after we did, Covid started. There was a reason why we did not feel peace about traditional schooling. As we followed the decision that brought us peace and not necessarily what we saw as convenient or logical, we avoided many of the frustrations that I heard other parents underwent that year. We had everything in place already, and the lockdowns did not interrupt our lives as much. God knew it and faithfully led us before it became an issue.

Homeschooling was a great blessing to our family for a few years. My son was able to skip a grade, I was able to complete my Masters in Bible and we all spent a lot of quality time together. That being said, there came a time in which homeschooling was not working for our family. The Lord was clearly calling me to write this book and I could not find the time to do it. I remember we even moved to a larger house with a yard and joined a homeschool group, but the frustrations kept rising. I could not find the solution to our schooling dilemma, one more time. I kept doing school tours and trying different homeschool approaches, but nothing felt right. I was overwhelmed. One day, after praying and praying and asking others for prayer, I just "impulsively" drove to the local Public School in March (two months before the end of the year) and asked for applications. I remember feeling like I was doing something wrong. I had heard about all the benefits of homeschooling and the warnings about Public Education. I felt like a failure, but I did not see any other way out. I was losing my temper more and more and it did not feel right.

Surprisingly enough, once again, the Lord made a way in an unexpected manner. They accepted my children right away; our peace came back and we had joy! The kids got great teachers and friends, and we were so thankful that we took that step.

It's been a little over a year since that day, and my kids have greatly benefited from attending Public School. My daughter learned how to read, something I had unsuccessfully tried at home and my son made friends and was awarded for his advanced math skills. The structure was also a blessing for us as a family. My youngest also started preschool and the Lord blessed her with an amazing principal who challenged her and led her to skip to an advanced class, something that I would have done if I was homeschooling.

Why am I telling this story? Because I want to assure someone that at the end of the day, the way forward might not look like what you expected, or what worked for others around you, but that's quite alright. It's not the specific program that guarantees victory for your children, but the Lord. As long as we follow His lead, we have nothing to fear. Whether it's Homeschooling, Unschooling, Private or Public education, you need to listen to the Lord and what's best for your family at that specific point in time, and also be open to changing back when needed. Nothing is set in stone, and that's ok too.

Today, thanks to that decision I am about to finish this book. I also realized that I was most likely burned out and needed this time to write and recharge. Only God could have led me to do this. I am now open to going back to Homeschooling them again if that's what the Lord wants; either way, God is always faithful. I had to be humble and accept my limitations and the fact that without God's blessing, I did not have the grace to do it. We can only accomplish what we are called to do. If something is not for us, it will only bring frustration. Do not look at what others are doing. Be confident in your ability to hear from the Lord and you will not fail.

Sometimes, we are hitting a wall in a specific area, and we don't know why. It might mean that we need to change directions, it might also mean that God has a fresh new way of doing that same thing, or it might mean we need to keep praying and persevere through that difficult season. That frustration might be there to tell us something. We need to determine the root cause of that frustration and follow what the Lord leads us to do about it instead. Isaiah 55:8-9 states (ESV):

"For my thoughts are not your thoughts,
neither are your ways my ways, declares the LORD.
For as the heavens are higher than the earth,
so are my ways higher than your ways
and my thoughts than your thoughts."

Let's consult the Lord before anyone else and be open to His direction, even when it does not look like what we had envisioned. He knows better, and we can trust Him.

Questions to Reflect

Do I have instances in my life in which I followed God's voice when it did not make sense and turned out to be a blessing?

_____
_____
_____

Do I ever fear what others will say if I step out in faith and obey what God is telling me to do?

_____
_____
_____

Do I trust that His intentions for me are good and His plans for me are better than anything I could plan for myself?

_____
_____
_____

Breakthrough Prayer

Thank you, Lord, that You know the end from the beginning. Please help me trust You with every decision in my life, knowing You will not let me fail. Please help me develop the confidence to hear Your voice instead of following what others around me would like me to do. Thank You for Your peace, which will confirm Your will. In Jesus' name. Amen.

Day Twenty-nine

Elimelech's Legacy

Elimelech and his sons Mahlon and Chilion had passed away, leaving Naomi and his two daughters-in-law, Orpah and Ruth, alone as widows. Proverbs 14:12 (ESV) states: *"There is a way that seems right to a man, but its end is the way to death."* Every decision we make bears consequences that can last a lifetime. This was the legacy that Elimelech left to his family.

Widows in Ancient Israel

Widows in ancient Israel were among the most vulnerable people in society. Men in the family were responsible for providing security to their wives and daughters. These three women were now left to fend for themselves. Once a woman became a widow, she would lose all social standing and be "generally without political or economic status."

Especially in rural areas, "women had little opportunity to pursue independent careers and were overwhelmingly dependent on their husbands for sustenance".[19] As explored earlier in our chapter about Hannah, women had significant roles in the household. The ideal woman in ancient Israel, as described in Proverbs 31, "provided both clothing and food for her family and servants, managed the estate, cared for the poor, sold their handwork, and engaged in teaching".[20] This was a lot of responsibility. Still, it was all done in the context of her household and her family. Naomi and her daughters-in-law did not have that option anymore.

Widows like Naomi could not inherit property from their husbands either. The land was typically passed down from father to son, and daughters could inherit land only if they married a relative. This was referred to as the "redeemer-kinsman legislation" (Leviticus 25:39-55), but because Naomi was past her child-bearing years, she was unlikely to get married again. Naomi was also living in a foreign land with no relatives, which reduced the likelihood of any help significantly. Widows with no male protector "were therefore economically dependent on society at large."[21] This was an extremely desperate situation for Naomi, as the only two options she would have had at this point were to "sell herself into slavery, to try to earn a living through prostitution, or to die of neglect."[22]

Throughout the Bible, however, we can see that God made provision for vulnerable people like orphans, foreigners, the poor, and the widows. It was part of God's commands for His people to care for the oppressed in society (Malachi 3:5). Apart from the mercy of God through the goodwill of strangers, women were at risk of being abused and exploited. Needless to say, the exploitation of widows was considered an atrocious crime.[23]

Naomi Took Action in the Midst of Her Desperate Moment (Ruth 1:6)

After 10 years of pain and suffering, a slither of hope rose up in Naomi as she overheard good news from her hometown:

> *"Then she arose with her daughters-in-law to return from the country of Moab, for she had heard in the fields of Moab that the LORD had visited his people and given them food" (ESV, Ruth 1:.6)*

As Naomi heard that the Lord had blessed her people, she did not hesitate to take action. She had no guarantees because of her age and her lack of status in society, but there must have been a point when she realized that Moab was not where the blessing of God was. Naomi was also able to discern that the good news she heard was an answer to her problems. Just like Jonah, when he recognized that the big fish was God's way to rescue him from death, she took that as a sign that not all hope was lost. She was willing to take the chance.

Life Lesson # 29:
Faith Plus Action

How often do we wait until we cannot find any other solution in sight before we start crying out to God or until we take steps towards something that we know we need to do? Naomi waited 10 years before she decided to return to where she was supposed to be. It took the loss of not only her husband but also her two sons for her to make the change she knew all along she was meant to make. This is likely why she took action as soon as she heard the news. She already knew what to do; that was just a confirmation. So, she took that word, left everything behind, and traveled on foot, putting her life and future on the line.

For some of us, our breakthrough will come when we make a decision we've been putting off, maybe out of fear

> **Our steps of faith "activate" the promises of God.**

or because we are still somewhat comfortable. What is the next step you know you need to take? Perhaps God has called you to start a ministry, enroll in Bible school, or move. Maybe it's as small as making a phone call or getting involved in your local church. For every person, it might take something different, but one thing I know is that your breakthrough is waiting on the other side of that decision. These actions towards what you know you should be doing are considered "steps of faith"; they are not necessarily going to make that miracle happen, but they are steps that prove to God that we truly believe His promises and we are willing to "partner" with Him to make them happen. Our steps of faith "activate" the promises of God.

I had "impossible" moments in which the only step of faith I could make was to apply for a job online that seemed unlikely to result in anything. But I did it, not because I believed that was enough to make that miracle happen, but because I knew how God works. His miracles start with our actions of faith. These small steps unlocked my miracle. I would take one tiny step, then another, then think of another, and the next thing you know, God would fill me up with faith and vision and direct me towards a much more significant breakthrough than I could have ever dreamed of. They are not always instantaneous; it might take many of those steps, but you will know, as you start walking, that God is behind those actions. He will fill you with His joy and expectation. Faith and obedience are two of the things God is most pleased with. Hebrews 11:6 states: *"And without faith, it is impossible to please God, because anyone who comes to him must believe that he exists and that he rewards those who earnestly seek him."*

1 Samuel 15:22 (ESV) states: *"Does the LORD delight in burnt offerings and sacrifices as much as in obeying the LORD? To obey is better than sacrifice, and to heed is better than the fat of rams."*

John 14:15 (ESV) states: *"If you love me, keep my commands."*

James 2:26 (ESV) states: *"As the body without the spirit is dead, so faith without deeds is dead."*

True faith manifests in actions, steps of faith, and obedience to God's directions. It might feel like a "small nudge" or a hint at first; you might not feel one hundred percent certain that was God speaking to you, but you choose to take that chance. That is faith. As you practice that childlike faith, your ears to His voice will get increasingly tuned in, and He will open doors that you never even dreamed possible.

Questions to Reflect

What specific areas am I believing God for a breakthrough?

_____
_____
_____

What steps of faith can I take to unlock God's blessings in those areas?

_____
_____
_____

Is there something I already know the Lord has placed in my heart to do and that I have been putting off?

_____
_____
_____

Breakthrough Prayer

Dear God, open my eyes to see what direction You are leading me to go. Help me not to fear, and show You my true faith by stepping out into the unknown. Help me to be obedient to your voice, even in the most seemingly "insignificant" aspects of my life and be able to experience the breakthrough and freedom You have prepared for me on the other side. Thank You for going with me and for never leaving me. In Jesus' name. Amen.

Day Thirty

Naomi Returns to God

Naomi had had enough of Moab. She had been living away from God, and it had only brought sorrow and pain. It took her over ten years to finally make this decision. Going back to Bethlehem meant going back to God. Once the opportunity knocked on her door, she took it without hesitation. Jesus shared the story of the Prodigal Son (Luke 15:11-32), who took his inheritance and walked away from his father, only to squander it and come back humiliated and empty-handed. The Father did not reject his son after this, nor did He question his poor decision; He instead celebrated his return, forgave him, and honored him in front of everyone. This is the way God responds when we come back to Him. It does not matter how far we've gone astray, how much we have messed up, or how much pain we have caused others. We are one decision away from being back on track, welcomed, honored, and blessed by Our Heavenly Father.

Ruth and Orpa Follow Naomi (Ruth 1:10-14)

"So she set out from the place where she was with her two daughters-in-law, and they went on the way to return to the land of Judah" (ESV, Ruth 1:7).

Naomi started heading towards Bethlehem, and her daughters-in-law followed her. We do not know how far they have been traveling, but they had packed everything and started their journey with the full intention of moving to Bethlehem with Naomi. This was a very kind gesture. They had the chance to return to their mother's houses and eventually get married again. Going with Naomi meant leaving their families, their culture, and the possibility of marriage behind. For Naomi, bringing them might have also felt like a huge responsibility. Because they were Moabites, they were most likely not going to be able to get married in Bethlehem and were going to live in poverty.[24] As much as she appreciated their good intentions, she did not think it was their best option and encouraged them to go back:

> *"But Naomi said to her two daughters-in-law, 'Go, return each of you to her mother's house. May the* Lord *deal kindly with you, as you have dealt with the dead and with me. The* Lord *grant that you may find rest, each of you in the house of her husband!' Then she kissed them, and they lifted up their voices and wept. And said to her, 'We will go back with you to your people'" (ESV, Ruth 1:8-10).*

Naomi thought of their well-being before hers. She treated them as she would a daughter. She was willing to be left alone, with all the vulnerabilities that it entailed for a widow, just so that her daughters-in-law could have a future. She did not make them feel guilty or pressure them to come with her. When she mentioned "mother's house" instead of father's house, this distinction was made in order to emphasize the "women's quarters of the home" where they would be able to start preparations for a new marriage.[25] She wanted them to go back and restart their lives because they were still young to do so!

After this warning from Naomi, Orpa and Ruth wept loudly. They must have realized the price they were paying for following her. Regardless of this, they decided to continue their journey with her. Once again, Naomi insisted on them going back:

"But Naomi said, 'Return home, my daughters. Why would you come with me? Am I going to have any more sons, who could become your husbands? Return home, my daughters; I am too old to have another husband. Even if I thought there was still hope for me—even if I had a husband tonight and then gave birth to sons— would you wait until they grew up? Would you remain unmarried for them? No, my daughters. It is more bitter for me than for you, because the LORD's hand has turned against me!' At this they wept aloud again. Then Orpah kissed her mother-in-law goodbye, but Ruth clung to her" (ESV, Ruth 1:11-14).

The Israelite Law had specific instructions to protect widows and to avoid leaving them to fend for themselves. Deuteronomy 25:5-6 states that if a man dies and leaves a widow, she must marry his brother, and their first son will carry on the deceased brother's name. Because Naomi's sons had passed away, so this law could not be fulfilled on either Orpah or Ruth. Naomi was not planning on having more children to perform this duty because she was older, and even if she did, it would take too long for the potential sons to grow up. This would have been the only hope for these women, so Naomi warned them against following her for this very reason. She also explained that the Lord's hand has turned against her, (v.13), implying that staying with her will most likely result in further hardship, not a blessing.[26]

The women "wept" because they were at a crossroads, and neither would be easy. They would either leave her beloved mother-in-law behind, vulnerable to the reality of widows and possibly never seeing her again, or follow her and miss out on the possibility of ever getting married and having a future for themselves. They were not only young (most likely in their twenties), but they also lived in a society where the "personhood of a woman was attached to her having a husband."[27]

Life Lesson # 30:
Everything Must Bow Down to God

We might find ourselves at a crossroads several times in our lives. It might be a seemingly small matter or a life-changing decision like these young widows were facing. Regardless, every time we choose, we say no to something else. But how do we know which one is the right choice? One of the things I've discovered in my life is that it is not so much about the decision itself but the heart behind the decision. The first thing we need to do is to check our motives. We must ensure that our hearts are fully surrendered to God and we are not holding anything back from him. Philippians 2:9-11 (ESV) states:

> *"Therefore God has highly exalted him and bestowed on him the name that is above every name, so that at the name of Jesus every knee should bow, in heaven and on earth and under the earth, and every tongue confess that Jesus Christ is Lord, to the glory of God the Father."*

Everything in our lives must bow to the name of Jesus—our jobs, careers, reputations, finances, relationships, talents, dreams, sleep, our physical bodies, and even the way we spend our time. This means that every decision must be based on pleasing God and doing what He wants us to do first and foremost. We don't need to make decisions based on fear or survival. Our decisions don't need to be based on how to satisfy our immediate needs. Matthew 6:31-33 (ESV) states:

> **Everything in our lives must bow to the name of Jesus—our jobs, careers, reputations, finances, relationships, talents, dreams, sleep, our physical bodies, and even the way we spend our time.**

"Therefore do not be anxious, saying, 'What shall we eat?' or 'What shall we drink?' or 'What shall we wear?' For the Gentiles seek after all these things, and your heavenly Father knows that you need them all. But seek first the kingdom of God and his righteousness, and all these things will be added to you."

When our main motivation is to serve and please God, our needs will be met as part of this "contract," it's like a partnership we have with God. As long as we seek His interests first, He will take care of our interests.

Personal Story: Busy Season Was Not an Excuse

I knew God had called me to ministry since I was a teenager in Argentina, but I did not know how, or when, or what to do to get there. I would pray and wait, but nothing was clear yet. I followed the Lord one step at a time, finished college, got married, and started homeschooling our children. Although I believed I was doing the will of God for my life, I kept wondering when it would be my time to step into my 'calling.' Had I missed the will of God for my life? Had I made a mistake that disqualified me from my calling? I wasn't sure, but I was determined to find out. My passion for God's work was strong, but I was unsure of what practical steps to take, especially as a busy mom and wife.

I remember I had recently moved, and we had gone through a long period of renovating our home. I was pretty obsessed with making my house "perfect," but the Lord started talking to me about 'His house.' I had been so consumed with my house that I had neglected being involved in His house. My marriage was suffering, and we needed God to be the center again. We used to pray regularly and attend church, but we had gotten so busy and entangled in our goals that God was no longer our main priority.

We hit a wall and decided that enough was enough; we would make the necessary changes to get back on track. Our home looked 'good enough,' and it did not need to be 'perfect.' House projects could wait, but our marriage and relationship with God could not. We then decided to attend a 'marriage ministry' called Re-Engage at our local church. It was inconvenient because it was late evening, and we had a toddler and a baby, but it did not matter. We wanted our breakthrough and would not get it from the comfort of our new leather couch at home.

We also joined the prayer group at church, and again, it took getting up earlier and leaving the kids in church for two services instead of one, but we were holding our 'side of the deal.' We wanted God to give us a breakthrough in our home; we had listen to His instructions and were showing Him we meant it. He was number one, not just in our thoughts and intentions, but in practice. We also decided to get marriage counseling at church, and we had to get a babysitter once a week for it, and arrange our schedules for it. I also decided to join a 'mom's group' once a week. There were no excuses. If the Lord had said to put His house first, then we would do that. He knows better and we desperately wanted His blessing over us!

This shift in our priorities happened at the right time. Eventually, a lady at the prayer group felt that I had to step out and help lead a group, so in faith, I volunteered to co-lead a group. As I was leading that group, the Lord firmly placed on my heart to study the Bible even more, so I enrolled in Bible School. It was while I was studying for my Masters in Bible that the Lord spoke to me about writing this book. I finally graduated a few years later, and now, over 7 years later, I am about to finish my first book and embark in a new journey serving the Lord through my writing. But it all started with small steps of obedience to His Word and small "inconveniences" and "discomforts" that showed God He was truly first. Serving Him, prioritizing His house, and being part of a community of believers all led to where I am today. It also helped our marriage tremendously. The community around us was also instrumental, while one of our daughters was hospitalized for a few weeks and needed surgery.

It might all start with a simple step of obedience to a seemingly small instruction from God, outside of any feelings, just a desire to obey Him. It might feel like a "sacrifice," but it will end up being the greatest decision of your life. You will never regret putting God first. It's time to take action. Get up and get moving towards God. That small first step of faith might make all the difference.

We can't wait for the ideal time to serve God; we can't wait until we are 'retired' to fully commit to God. Our love and commitment to God need to be reflected in tangible ways today. He will give us the grace to do it, and will increase our capacity as we move forward in obedience.

Something I do want to address is that there are seasons of preparation where God might not want us to be involved in ministry just yet, which is just as legitimate. We need to figure out what season we are in.

Personal Story: Times of Preparation

As a sophomore student-athlete, I was so eager to serve God that I started leading a Bible study, attending the leadership meetings, evangelizing on Friday nights, and going to every Chapel and church service offered on campus, plus a different church on Sunday. Then my grades started to suffer, and the Lord spoke to me about taking a break from that many commitments because my main calling at that time was to study. This " preparation " time was not very exciting in itself; it took discipline and hard work, and quite honestly, it felt pretty mundane and boring, but that was the season I was in.

A similar scenario happened when my son was 18 months old, and I was offered a job as the Director of Children's Ministry on one of our Church campuses. It seemed ideal because I could bring my son to work, but the Lord directed me against it. He had other priorities for me at that time. I was to serve Him, but not in that capacity yet. We were still building our family, and that was my priority.

I'm sharing these two contrasting personal experiences to point out that there is grace for any season you might be in. There are different seasons in life. We need to have discernment and understand our current season.

Everyone is in a different season in their walk with the Lord, and we should not fall into the trap of comparing ourselves to others or even judging other people who might not be called to the same task or assignment as us. 2 Corinthians 10:12-13 (ESV) talks about the foolishness of comparing ourselves to one another:

> *"Not that we dare to classify or compare ourselves with some of those who are commending themselves. But when they measure themselves by one another and compare themselves with one another, they are without understanding. But we will not boast beyond limits, but will boast only with regard to the area of influence God assigned to us, to reach even to you."*

Let's be faithful to the things God has entrusted us with today. God will lead us to more significant things as we steward them well.

Questions to Reflect

What season in life am I in right now? Preparation? Ministry? Am I walking in a season of waiting, where I need to continue walking in faith and not give up?

Are there any specific actions the Lord is leading me to take to grow in Him today?

Do I feel led to study His Word further, step out in faith in a specific area, serve him in some capacity, share my testimony with others, or help someone in need?

Breakthrough Prayer

Lord, help me make decisions that reflect Your main priority in my life. Everything in my schedule, my finances, and my heart is Yours. Thank You. As long as I please You first, my needs will be covered. In Jesus' name. Amen.

Day Thirty-one

RUTH COMMITS HER LIFE FULLY TO GOD
(RUTH 1:16-18)

After considering the reality of this choice, one of the two daughters-in-law, Orpah, decided to go back with her family. We should not blame her. She had her whole life in front of her and had the right to make that verdict. On the other hand, Ruth boldly decided to continue the journey. Relentlessly, Naomi tried once more to convince her to return: *"'Look,' said Naomi, 'your sister-in-law is going back to her people and her gods. Go back with her'" (ESV, Ruth 1:15)*. Ruth was not only a widow but was about to become a foreigner in Israel. Naomi could not stress the severity of this situation more. However, Ruth spoke up with determination after that last attempt, and Naomi never brought it up again. Ruth was aware of the cost of her decision and decided to go forward regardless:

> *"But Ruth replied, 'Don't urge me to leave you or to turn back from you. Where you go I will go, and where you stay I will stay. Your people will be my people and your God my God. Where you die I will die, and there I will be buried. May the LORD deal with me, be it ever so severely, if even death separates you and me.' When Naomi realized that Ruth was determined to go with her, she stopped urging her'"* (NIV, Ruth 1:16-18).

Ruth's words were more than just good intentions. According to tradition, this declaration was a well-thought-out "covenant."[28] This was a "unilateral verbal contract." She decided to forsake her land, people, religion, and any hope for her future, even if it lead to death. When she said, "Your people will be my people and your God my God," these words echoed God's Words throughout the Hebrew Bible, declaring His covenant with Israel. This "divine pledge" is usually referred to by scholars as a "covenant formula," so by doing this, Ruth was invoking the same covenant with God as if she were an Israelite. Ruth's commitment to Naomi has been compared to that of Abraham. She left her land, people, culture, and religion and committed to God and Naomi, without knowing precisely what the future would hold. In contrast to Abraham, who was holding on to great promises from God, she only expected tragedy. She expressed this commitment as a formal oath that bound her to Naomi until death.[29]

Ruth's covenant is peculiar in that she was not an Israelite. At this point in history, Israel was the only nation God had chosen for Himself; all others did not have this privilege yet. However, some exceptions in the Old Testament demonstrated that Gentiles could be converted if they genuinely believed. One of these examples was the sailors in Jonah's story (Jonah 1:14-15) who cried out to God.

Ruth's faith and commitment to God and His people were considered signs of conversion. We will see later how God was pleased with this covenant and, as a result, included Ruth, even though she was not an Israelite by birth, in His plan for humanity.

Life Lesson # 31:
The Lord Cares for the Oppressed in Society

Plenty of passages in the Old and the New Testament demonstrate God's heart for the most vulnerable in society. He commands His people to include them in their activities and feasts, makes provision for them, and condemns those who dare to take advantage of them.

The Bible even refers to God as the "Father of the fatherless" and "Defender of widows."

Deuteronomy 10:17-19 (NIV) states:

"For the LORD your God is God of gods and Lord of lords, the great God, mighty and awesome, who shows no partiality and accepts no bribes. He defends the cause of the fatherless and the widow, and loves the foreigner residing among you, giving them food and clothing. And you are to love those who are foreigners, for you yourselves were foreigners in Egypt."

Further instructions on how to follow through in this command are explained in Deuteronomy 24:14-22. In Jeremiah 7:5-7 (NIV) we see the same concept and how much God values those who follow those commands:

"If you really change your ways and your actions and deal with each other justly, if you do not oppress the foreigner, the fatherless or the widow and do not shed innocent blood in this place, and if you do not follow other gods to your own harm, then I will let you live in this place, in the land I gave your ancestors for ever and ever."

In Malachi 3:5 (NIV) we see how God condemns those who oppress the disadvantages alongside the worst of sinners:

"'So I will come to put you on trial. I will be quick to testify against sorcerers, adulterers and perjurers, against those who defraud laborers of their wages, who oppress the widows and the fatherless, and deprive the foreigners among you of justice, but do not fear me,' says the Lord Almighty."

Psalm 68:5-6 (NIV) describes God as:

*"A father to the fatherless, a defender of widows,
is God in his holy dwelling.
God sets the lonely in families, he leads out the prisoners with singing;
but the rebellious live in a sun-scorched land."*

And Psalm 146:9 (NIV) states:

*"The LORD watches over the foreigner
and sustains the fatherless and the widow,
but he frustrates the ways of the wicked."*

Finally, in the New Testament, the book of James 1:27 (NIV) clarifies what are those good works that God holds in high esteem:

"Religion that God our Father accepts as pure and faultless is this: to look after orphans and widows in their distress and to keep oneself from being polluted by the world."

God's view of those struggling is that of a loving father. He is compassionate and ready to answer those who call on him and help them. He is always prepared to listen and come to their help. He does not look at people by the color of their skin, nationality, or position in the church or society. He does not even look at our past; as long as we genuinely come to Him, He is ready to forgive us and turn our lives around.

Questions to Reflect

Is there anyone in my path who is vulnerable and might need my help?

_____

_____

_____

Is there anything I can share with the less fortunate, whether it might be time, resources, or talents?

_____

_____

_____

What is usually my attitude towards those who are struggling? Am I critical of their situation? Do I show compassion and kindness? Am I willing to be inconvenienced in order to help others?

_____

_____

_____

Do I actively look for ways to help those who are in desperate situations? Or perhaps, am I the one who desperately needs help today?

_____

_____

_____

Breakthrough Prayer

Dear Lord, thank You for caring for those in vulnerable positions. Help me find ways to help those in need and, in doing so, reflect Your compassionate heart to this world. Show me those people You have already placed in my path that I could help. If I ever find myself in a leadership position, help me to be fair and never take advantage of those who depend on me. In Jesus' name. Amen.

Day Thirty-two

The Journey to Bethlehem: It Took Action
(Ruth 1:19-22)

"So the two women went on until they came to Bethlehem. When they arrived in Bethlehem, the whole town was stirred because of them, and the women exclaimed, 'Can this be Naomi?'

"'Don't call me Naomi,' she told them. 'Call me Mara, because the Almighty has made my life very bitter. I went away full, but the Lord has brought me back empty. Why call me Naomi? The Lord has afflicted me; the Almighty has brought misfortune upon me.'

"So Naomi returned from Moab accompanied by Ruth the Moabite, her daughter-in-law, arriving in Bethlehem as the barley harvest was beginning." (NIV, Ruth 1:19-22)

Naomi's repentant heart was manifested in her actions. The trip back to Bethlehem took courage and humility. Her expectations for this return were not inspiring. She had been humbled by the tragic death of her husband and sons, her lack of grandchildren, and her status as a widow. She had adopted the pain and misfortune as part of her identity, to the point that she wanted others to refer to her as "Mara," which in the Hebrew language means "bitter"[30] instead of Naomi, which means "pleasant."[31] The trip back to Bethlehem had not been easy. She likely had to leave most of her possessions behind and embark on a journey on foot that took several days. She had experienced nothing but pain for the past ten years.

Naomi also felt like God had punished her through the death of her husband and sons. Because widows were vulnerable in those days, she did not know how things would turn out. She believed that God would provide for her, but her expectations for the future were low. After everything she had gone through, she was content to be back and have her basic needs met. She did not expect anything special from the Lord.

Life Lesson # 32:
Don't Reference the Past—He is Doing Something New

How many times do we equate our past with our future? If we have had pain and struggles, we assume that will be our portion in the future. Some will even take some tragic event and turn it into a "badge" of honor. They share it with everyone. They use it as an excuse. They hide behind it and use it to justify their fruitlessness, lack of joy, and bitter attitude.

Life can be painful, and grief can most likely be debilitating. God sees the pain and cares. He never intended us to carry it with us. He wants to take our sorrow and turn it into joy! Psalm 30:11-12 (NIV) states:

> *"You turned my wailing into dancing;*
> *you removed my sackcloth and clothed me with joy,*
> *that my heart may sing your praises and not be silent.*
> *Lord my God, I will praise you forever."*

Grief is a natural response to tragedy and loss. However, there is a point at which we must move forward. There is a verse that the

Lord has given me throughout the years so that I do not dwell in the past. I often get stuck in a particular season of life, assuming that, from now on, this is the way life will be. But the Lord keeps reminding me that as long as I follow Him, life will never be on repeat. He is constantly creating, re-creating, renewing us, and doing something new in our lives. We have to let go of the old to make room for it! Whether glorious or tragic, the past is in the past and must remain there. Isaiah 43:18-19 (NIV) states:

> *"Forget the former things;*
> *do not dwell on the past.*
> *See, I am doing a new thing!*
> *Now it springs up; do you not perceive it?*
> *I am making a way in the wilderness*
> *and streams in the wasteland."*

God sympathizes with our pain but does not want us to stay there. He has the power to turn any misfortune into a testimony. If we surrender it to Him, He can turn those painful memories into a legacy.

Questions to Reflect

Have I encountered injustices in my life?

Who has disappointed me, rejected me, violated my trust, or caused me pain?

Am I willing to surrender it all to the Lord, knowing that God can make all the wrongs, right?

Do I trust that God not only cares for me but will even make restitution for all the pain and loss I've experienced?

Breakthrough Prayer

Dear God, please take my past experiences, disappointments, injustices, and pain I have experienced and trade them for your freedom, deliverance, forgiveness, and joy. I surrender any injustices to you, trusting You will fight those battles for me and show me the way forward. As I let go of the past and trust You with my future, please use all the hardships for my good, uproot any bitterness in my soul, and fill me with the sweet taste of your un-relentless love for me! Thank You for a bright future. Thank You for your purposes being fulfilled in my life, and thank You for your abundant life and overflowing joy in my heart. I am yours fully. In Jesus' name. Amen.

Day Thirty-three

Proof of Repentance

Naomi took action, which proved to God that she had a change of heart. She believed God would provide for her if she returned to her land. We do not have an account of a specific prayer of repentance, but her trip back to Bethlehem was proof. As the story unfolds, we will discover how God took notice of her actions and rewarded her openly and abundantly for them.

Life Lesson #33:
God Rewards Obedience, Not Perfection

Hebrews 11:6 (NIV) states:

> "And without faith it is impossible to please God, because anyone who comes to him must believe that he exists and that he rewards those who earnestly seek him."

God rewards those who seek Him and follow His ways. Naomi's story demonstrates how one act of obedience, one decision in the right direction, can turn years of disobedience around. God is merciful and patient and takes notice when we move towards Him.

Romans 5:18-19 (NIV) proves this point by explaining what Jesus did for us on the cross:

"Consequently, just as one trespass resulted in condemnation for all people, so also one righteous act resulted in justification and life for all people. For just as through the disobedience of the one man the many were made sinners, so also through the obedience of the one man the many will be made righteous."

Adam disobeyed and brought a curse on humanity, but Jesus's obedience in dying on the cross made salvation available to all. In the same manner, we can contrast Elimelech and Naomi. Elimelech brought his family to a pagan nation in direct disobedience to God's commands and brought death and much pain to his family. On the other hand, when Naomi decided to return to God, we will soon find out that God rewarded her obedience and restored her and her descendants significantly.

Questions to Reflect

Do I ever struggle with feeling that I'm not good enough?

Do I ever feel like God will not accept me because I am not "perfect" yet?

If so, is this discouragement keeping me from taking steps of faith and obedience, thinking they won't matter anyway?

Breakthrough Prayer

Thank You, Lord, that You are willing and ready to take me back, no matter what my past may look like. Thank You that You are not looking for perfect people but those who turn to You in faith. Help me to take steps of faith and obedience today, knowing that You will reward me openly. Help me open my heart and receive those blessings and rewards You send me, without guilt, shame or condemnation. In Jesus' name. Amen.

Day Thirty-four

The Process Before the Miracle (Ruth 2:1-9)

"Now Naomi had a relative of her husband, a man of great wealth, of the family of Elimelech, whose name was Boaz. And Ruth the Moabitess said to Naomi, 'Please let me go to the field and glean among the ears of grain following one in whose eyes I may find favor.' And she said to her, 'Go, my daughter.' So she left and went and gleaned in the field after the reapers; and she happened to come to the portion of the field belonging to Boaz, who was of the family of Elimelech. Now behold, Boaz came from Bethlehem and said to the reapers, 'May the Lord be with you.' And they said to him, 'May the Lord bless you.' Then Boaz said to his servant who was in charge of the reapers, 'Whose young woman is this?' And the servant in charge of the reapers replied, 'She is the young Moabite woman who returned with Naomi from the land of Moab. And she said, 'Please let me glean and gather after the reapers among the sheaves.' So she came and has remained from the morning until now; she has been sitting in the house for a little while.'"

"Then Boaz said to Ruth, 'Listen carefully, my daughter. Do not go to glean in another field; furthermore, do not go on from this one, but join my young women here. Keep your eyes on the field which they reap, and go after them. Indeed, I have ordered the servants not to touch you. When you are thirsty, go to the water jars and drink from what the servants draw'" (NASB, Ruth 2:1-9).

"Ruth requested that Naomi allow her to go into the fields to pick up [or glean] the leftover grain." God's law expressly allowed the poor the right to glean in the fields:

"When you reap the harvest of your land, moreover, you shall not reap to the very edges of your field nor gather the gleaning of your harvest; you are to leave them for the needy and the stranger. I am the LORD your God" (NASB, Leviticus 23:22).

However, the owners of the fields were not always cooperative. Ruth was aware of the reality of how "the poor and the foreigner were treated by hostile landowners."[32]

Boaz was considered a "man of standing," which meant either a "good warrior or a distinguished, honored person."[33] The fact that he asked, "Whose young woman is that?" suggests an attraction to Ruth, a woman he had not noticed previously working in his fields. Because of their culture, this question indicates that he was seeking information about her ancestry or clan[34]. Boaz had heard about Naomi and Ruth but had not yet met them. The report about Ruth was positive, describing her as hard-working. This is how the Lord arranged to provide for Ruth and Naomi. They obtained favor with the landowner through someone else's testimony. This is similar to when Joseph was introduced to Pharaoh by the cupbearer, and he got promoted as a result. (Genesis 41:1-45) In both cases, they were doing the right thing in private, but the Lord appointed somebody to notice them to bless them and get them where they needed to go.

When Boaz heard the report, his interest in her increased, and he ordered the men not to 'touch' her. He also gave her special privileges like drinking from the water jars, which was usually not permitted to "gleaners."[35]

He not only invited her to stay in the field, but he also put around her his cloak of protection. He said, "I have now given orders that you can come into this field and that you will not be hurt or harmed in any way." Frankly, on that day, it was very dangerous for a woman in Ruth's position—a widow from Moab. She was likely to have insult upon insult heaped upon her. Not only that, but she would not be safe. Boaz, recognizing that immediately put his cloak of protection around her. It was almost as unsafe on the roads of Bethlehem on that day as it would be today on the streets of our modern cities.

Life Lesson # 34: Don't Give Up; It's a Process

In the Bible, God often provides, heals, and even delivers His people through a process. A miracle is not always instantaneous. By faith, we have what we asked for the moment we prayed:

> *"This is the confidence which we have before Him, that, if we ask anything according to His will, He hears us. And if we know that He hears us in whatever we ask, we know that we have the requests which we have asked from Him" (NASB, 1 John 5:14-15).*

God often chooses a unique process in which we must exercise our faith to see the full manifestation of that miracle. You may ask God for a job, but He might lead you to go back to school and study first, then create a resume, apply for many jobs, and show up to interviews, only to them provide a "divine" connection at the last minute that makes that specific miracle happen. We have a part to play in our miracle. That part is the proof that we believe. We might not know precisely how God will do it, but that is not our job. Our job is to obey what is right according to His Word and follow His lead one step at a time.

When the Lord led me to enroll in Bible School, I had two small children and did not know where I would get the time to study. But I listened, obeyed, and registered by faith. Once I was accepted, I found out that my husband and I were expecting our third child. I remember getting discouraged, feeling that there was no way I would ever find time to study for this Degree! Little did I know that the World was about to shut down due to COVID-19, and my husband, a pilot, would be home a lot more often than not, making it possible for us to arrange our schedule for me to study.

The same scenario happened many times during the last 25 years of walking with the Lord. When He led me to start writing this book, I was homeschooling, we were moving, and renovating our new home among other things. But I remember sitting down and starting by faith, one page at a time. I did not know how on earth I would ever get the time to finish it. Once more, He made a way, but it did not happen until I started moving forward, regardless of how our circumstances looked like. I did not wait for everything to be "ideal" to answer the call. I went for it, and He provided it as I went. The more we learn to obey God's voice, even when in the natural it seems impossible, the easier it will get to trust Him, and the quicker we will watch Him move.

> **The more we learn to obey God's voice, even when in the natural it seems impossible, the easier it will get to trust Him, and the quicker we will watch Him move.**

Let's take a look at Psalm 40:6-8 (AMP) for example:

"Sacrifice and meal offering You do not desire, nor do You delight in them;
You have opened my ears and given me the capacity to hear [and obey Your word];
Burnt offerings and sin offerings You do not require.
Then I said, 'Behold, I come [to the throne];
In the scroll of the book it is written of me.'
"I delight to do Your will, O my God;

Your law is within my heart."

This verse was meant to correct the idea that the "sacrificial system worked automatically, apart from expressing faith, repentance, and obedience."[36] Sacrifices on their own do not produce any blessings. The Lord is seeking "an open ear." Those ready to listen to Him and do what He says will be blessed. Let's look at Hebrews 11, for example. This is a beautiful chapter and is often cited in regard to faith. It lists several Old Testament heroes who lived by faith, and by doing so, they pleased God:

"Now faith is confidence in what we hope for and assurance about what we do not see. This is what the ancients were commended for.

By faith we understand that the universe was formed at God's command, so that what is seen was not made out of what was visible.

By faith Abel brought God a better offering than Cain did. By faith he was commended as righteous when God spoke well of his offerings. And by faith Abel still speaks, even though he is dead.

By faith Enoch was taken from this life, so that he did not experience death: "He could not be found, because God had taken him away." For before he was taken, he was commended as one who pleased God. 6 And without faith it is impossible to please God, because anyone who comes to him must believe that he exists and that he rewards those who earnestly seek him.

By faith Noah, when warned about things not yet seen, in holy fear built an ark to save his family. By his faith he condemned the world and became heir of the righteousness that is in keeping with faith.

By faith Abraham, when called to go to a place he would later receive as his inheritance, obeyed and went, even though he did not know where he was going. By faith he made his home in the Promised Land like a stranger in a foreign country; he lived in tents, as did Isaac and Jacob, who were heirs with him of the same promise. For he was looking forward to the city with foundations, whose architect and builder is God. And by faith even Sarah, who was past childbearing age, was enabled to bear children because she considered him faithful who had made the promise. And so from this one man, and he as good as dead, came descendants as numerous as the stars in the sky and as countless as the sand on the seashore" (ESV, Hebrews 11:1-12).

Faith must be accompanied by action, just as much as action must be motivated by faith to be effective. James 2:14-19 (**NIV**) states:

"What good is it, my brothers and sisters, if someone claims to have faith but has no deeds? Can such faith save them? Suppose a brother or a sister is without clothes and daily food. If one of you says to them, 'Go in peace; keep warm and well fed,' but does nothing about their physical needs, what good is it? In the same way, faith by itself, if it is not accompanied by action, is dead.

But someone will say, 'You have faith; I have deeds.'

Show me your faith without deeds, and I will show you my faith by my deeds. You believe that there is one God. Good! Even the demons believe that—and shudder."

As we can see in these examples, it's not perfection nor rituals that provoke God's blessings, but it's our faith manifested in actions. If we were to look at every one of the people listed in Hebrews 11, we would find out that none of them were perfect. Just like Naomi, many had made some major mistakes, but it was their faith that made them eligible to be used by God. Nothing else.

Questions to Reflect

Do I ever disqualify myself based on my background or past failures?

_____

_____

_____

Have I ever felt like I don't belong in God's family? Have I ever been rejected or "left out" because of my past?

_____

_____

_____

Am I willing to start treating others, and myself, based on what God says and not based on human standards?

_____

_____

_____

Breakthrough Prayer

Dear God, help me receive your forgiveness, love, and acceptance. Also, please help me not to allow the opinions of others, or even my thoughts, to attempt to tarnish my true identity in you. Thank You for your unconditional acceptance and complete forgiveness. Thank You that I am a new Creation in Christ and a co-heir in Him; nobody can take that away from me. Help me walk as the free son or daughter of the King that I am, without shame or condemnation from my past. In Jesus' name. Amen.

Day Thirty-five

Interaction Between Ruth and Boaz (Ruth 2:10-16)

"Then she fell on her face, bowing to the ground, and said to him, 'Why have I found favor in your sight that you should take notice of me, since I am a foreigner?' Boaz replied to her, 'All that you have done for your mother-in-law after the death of your husband has been fully reported to me, and how you left your father and your mother and the land of your birth, and came to a people that you did not previously know. May the Lord reward your work, and may your wages be full from the Lord, the God of Israel, under whose wings you have come to take refuge.' Then she said, 'I have found favor in your sight, my lord, for you have comforted me and indeed have spoken kindly to your servant, though I am not like one of your female servants.'

And at mealtime Boaz said to her, 'Come here, that you may eat of the bread and dip your piece of bread in the vinegar.' So she sat beside the reapers; and he served her roasted grain, and she ate and was satisfied and had some left. When she got up to glean, Boaz commanded his servants, saying, 'Let her glean even among the sheaves, and do not insult her. Also you are to purposely slip out for her some grain from the bundles and leave it so that she may glean, and do not rebuke her'" (NASB, Ruth 2:10-16).

They arrived "as the barley harvest was beginning." According to Jewish law, this was the perfect setup for Ruth to glean among the fields and, as a foreign woman, gather some food. It also indicates that the food shortage was over. Ruth gleaned in the fields of a relative who decided to be kind and generous to her and included her in the harvest along with other young women to protect her.

Boaz did not recognize Ruth, but he had heard of her. He had heard positive things about her. He knew of her kindness to Naomi and how she had left her land, family, and people to be with Naomi. God made a way for her to end up in that particular field. He had also made provision for Boaz to show up at the right time and to have heard of her in a positive light before.

According to ancient Near Eastern culture, Ruth's response to Boaz's kindness reflected her gratitude and humility. She "bowed" herself with her face to the ground before him and asked in amazement why she, a foreigner, had found favor in his eyes.[37] She did not expect to be treated well as a foreign woman of Moab, much less to be given protection and abundant provision.

Life Lesson # 35:
Expect Far More Than You Asked For

This "coincidence" in the story was not an accident. This is where the plans of God started to unfold. Often, we limit God to be a "supplier of needs." We come to him expecting "just enough" to get by, to make it another day. However, his purposes far surpass those of the day-to-day. He desires to use our lives for eternal purposes. He wishes to work in our hearts and transform our lives from the inside out. We might initially go to God because we have a pressing need, but we will discover that as we continue drawing closer to Him, He will meet those needs, but He will go a lot further than that. Romans 8:28-29 (NIV) states:

"And we know that God causes all things to work together for good to those who love God, to those who are called according to His purpose. For those whom He foreknew, He also predestined to become conformed to the image of His Son, so that He would be the firstborn among many brothers and sisters."

Our hearts are sometimes fixed on the temporary affairs of life. God, on the other hand, even though He is concerned about our daily lives and cares for every detail of it, He is looking at the big picture. He has a purpose for our lives, and He is using everything we go through, even the pain and the suffering, to bring it to fruition. He is also transforming us into the Image of Christ. We are to reflect the new nature we received when we were born again, and all the hardships we endure serve as tools to accomplish that very purpose. Romans 5:3-5 (ESV) states:

"...we rejoice in our sufferings, knowing that suffering produces endurance, and endurance produces character, and character produces hope, and hope does not put us to shame, because God's love has been poured into our hearts through the Holy Spirit who has been given to us."

That being said, God is not sending us hardships, but He takes those sufferings and every tear we shed and puts them to good use. 2 Timothy 1:8-9 (ESV) states:

"Therefore do not be ashamed of the testimony about our Lord, nor of me his prisoner, but share in suffering for the gospel by the power of God, who saved us and called us to a holy calling, not because of our works but because of his own purpose and grace, which he gave us in Christ Jesus before the ages began."

Psalm 57:2 (ESV) states:

*"I cry out to God Most High,
to God who fulfills his purpose for me."*

He can take the biggest disappointments in life and turn them into a powerful testimony.

Naomi and Ruth made the right decision to go back to Bethlehem. They left everything behind and came humbly with no guarantees of provision of any kind. But God took notice and made a way for them, above and beyond what they could have asked or expected. Ephesians 3:20-21 (ESV) states:

"Now to him who is able to do immeasurably more than all we ask or imagine, according to his power that is at work within us, to him be glory in the church and in Christ Jesus throughout all generations, for ever and ever! Amen."

God was not only providing for their basic needs. He also had an excellent plan that exceeded their needs and expectations—a plan tied to an eternal purpose.

Questions to Consider

When I pray about a situation I am facing, do I ever consider the eternal purposes behind it?

What would I like God to do for me in the next six months to a year?

Am I willing to pray for not only my needs to be met and my desires fulfilled but, most importantly, that His purposes be revealed and fulfilled through the trials I might be facing?

Am I willing to surrender to God during the periods of trials and persevere even when I do not see the reason behind the suffering, knowing that a greater purpose will eventually be unfolded?

Breakthrough Prayer

Thank you, Lord, that You are always listening. Thank You for caring for me and for being able to supply my every need. I surrender all my needs and wants today and every trial I might face. I thank You that You will turn everything I have encountered in my past and what I am facing today for my good. Thank You for orchestrating life events and difficulties so that You can fulfill Heaven's purposes in my life, and one day, it will all make sense. Please help me to trust You in the process. Please help me to live with a sense of expectation of the beautiful plans You have for me. In Jesus' name. Amen.

Day Thirty-six

Ruth Shares the News with Naomi
(Ruth 2:17-23)

"So she gleaned in the field until evening. Then she beat out what she had gleaned, and it was about an ephah of barley. And she picked it up and went into the city, and her mother-in-law saw what she had gleaned. She also took some out and gave Naomi what she had left after she was satisfied. Her mother-in-law then said to her, 'Where did you glean today and where did you work? May he who took notice of you be blessed.' So she told her mother-in-law with whom she had worked, and said, 'The name of the man with whom I worked today is Boaz.' Naomi said to her daughter-in-law, 'May he be blessed of the Lord who has not withdrawn His kindness from the living and from the dead.' Again Naomi said to her, 'The man is our relative; he is one of our redeemers.' Then Ruth the Moabitess said, 'Furthermore, he said to me, "You are to stay close to my servants until they have finished all my harvest."' And Naomi said to her daughter-in-law Ruth, 'It is good, my daughter, that you go out with his young women, so that others do not assault you in another field.' So she stayed close by the young women of Boaz in order to glean until the end of the barley harvest and the wheat harvest. And she lived with her mother-in-law" (NASB, Ruth 2:17-23).

Naomi's attitude changed right away when she heard the news. Her eyes were opened to what God had in store. Suddenly, she could see God's purpose in all of this. She understood that the favor that Ruth had received from Boaz was not ordinary. Just a few days earlier, she had warned Ruth about the hardships of being a poor foreigner without hopes of a husband, but today, the tone in her voice changes. She had a smile on her face and excitement in her voice. She was now filled with joy and expectation for the future!

Naomi was filled with hope and excitement because she knew who Boaz was; she understood the intricacies of the Jewish Law and could see what a miracle this encounter was. According to the Jewish landownership laws, only a relative from their clan was allowed to "redeem" the land that Elimelech had left in Bethlehem before they moved to Moab during the famine. Elimelech might have abandoned the land during the famine, or less likely, he would have sold it. Regardless of what he did with the land, the laws allowed the next of kin to repurchase it so it would remain in the family.[37] This was a blessing from God but not a guarantee yet. Boaz could potentially become the answer to these widows' problems, but he had to be willing to do it.

Life Lesson # 36:
God's Blessings are Comprehensive

Every detail of Ruth's report to Naomi seemed good. Proverbs 10:22 (ESV) states, *"The blessing of the Lord makes one rich, And He adds no sorrow with it."* When something comes from God, every detail is accounted for. In this case, not only did Ruth have abundant provisions, but she also had the protection she needed. Everything made sense, and this is the type of blessing that the Lord brings. He does not just provide for our immediate needs; He sees beyond our needs and provides even for those things we have not requested. His blessings are so great that eventually they overflow onto others:

Jeremiah 17:7-8 (NASB) says:

"Blessed is the man who trusts in the LORD,
And whose trust is the LORD.
For he will be like a tree planted by the water
That extends its roots by a stream,
And does not fear when the heat comes;
But its leaves will be green,
And it will not be anxious in a year of drought,
Nor cease to yield fruit."

Psalm 34:8 (NASB) states:

"Taste and see that the LORD is good;
How blessed is the man who takes refuge in Him!"

Naomi was not expecting much because of the pain she had experienced; her hope was nearly lost. Many times, when we experience pain and suffering, we tend to lose hope altogether. We start identifying with our pain and thinking this is "just the way things are," but the Lord is not done with our story. His purposes go beyond what we can comprehend, and He can turn the most impossible situation into the most significant victory of our lives. Jeremiah 29:11: *"For I know the plans that I have for you,' declares the LORD, 'plans for prosperity and not for disaster, to give you a future and a hope"*. The Lord made way for Ruth to encounter Boaz and find favor in his eyes to obtain food and protection, but it was not the end of the story; it was only the beginning. God had even more in store for these women, a lot more. He was about to turn their sorrow into dancing and their sadness into joy. King David, in Psalm 30 (ESV), described it this way:

*"Sing praise to the L*ORD*, you His godly ones,*
And praise the mention of His holiness.
For His anger is but for a moment,
His favor is for a lifetime;
Weeping may last for the night,
But a shout of joy comes in the morning" (Psalm 30:4-5).

"You have turned my mourning into dancing for me;
You have untied my sackcloth and encircled me with joy,
That my soul may sing praise to You and not be silent.
*L*ORD *my God, I will give thanks to You forever"* (Psalm 30:11-12).

Questions to Consider

Is there any area of my life in which I find it hard to hold on to hope?

Have I experienced at least one time in my life or someone close to me, when God made a way in a seemingly impossible situation? Do I believe He can do it once again?

Do I believe that God not only hears me and cares about my needs, but He wants to bless me abundantly and restore joy into my life?

Breakthrough Prayer

Thank you, Lord, for Your all-encompassing love for me. Thank You that You will my deepest sufferings and turn them into the greatest joy of my life. Restore hope, faith, expectation, and joy into my life. I want my life to become a testimony of your immense goodness and that it will overflow unto others around me. I love You, Lord. In Jesus' name. Amen.

Day Thirty-seven

Ruth and Naomi Move in Faith (Ruth 3:1-18)

"One day Ruth's mother-in-law Naomi said to her, 'My daughter, I must find a home for you, where you will be well provided for'" (ESV, Ruth 3:1).

Naomi had realized that when Ruth and Boaz had met, this was most likely a divine appointment. She was expectant, but time had passed, and Boaz had not made any moves yet. The Bible does not explicitly state why Boaz did not approach Ruth. Perhaps he was being respectful of her. She was younger and attractive, and he might not have been sure if he was interested in him. Given that she was very vulnerable, he might have chosen to respect her and not make her feel uncomfortable or pressured to do so. He had provided a safe place to "glean" and was not requiring any special favors in return.

Naomi understood Jewish customs and considered that Ruth should show Boaz that she was interested in him under the given circumstances. She then gave her particular instructions on how to do it properly to avoid being misinterpreted:

"Now then, is Boaz not our relative, with whose young women you were? Behold, he is winnowing barley at the threshing floor tonight. Wash yourself therefore, and anoint yourself, and put on your best clothes, and go down to the threshing floor; but do not reveal yourself to the man until he has finished eating and drinking. And it shall be when he lies down,

that you shall take notice of the place where he lies, and you shall go and uncover his feet and lie down; then he will tell you what you should do" (NASB, Ruth 3:2-4).

Naomi knew the Jewish culture and customs very well. She instructed Ruth precisely how to proceed so that she was understood. This was a very risky move on her part. As a foreigner especially, she ran the risk of being misjudged. She was to meet Boaz in private when other people could not see it so that she could keep her reputation and his intact.

"And she said to her, 'All that you say I will do.'

So she went down to the threshing floor and did according to all that her mother-in-law had commanded her. When Boaz had eaten and drunk and his heart was cheerful, he went to lie down at the end of the heap of grain; and she came secretly, and uncovered his feet and lay down" (NASB, Ruth 3:5-7).

Ruth was taking a risk by approaching a man in the dark while he was sleeping; she was risking her reputation and her safety. Due to her low status, starting a conversation with Boaz in broad daylight would not have been appropriate for her. Boaz was a respected man, and it would have risked his reputation to speak with her in front of others. However, if anyone saw them at night, they would also have assumed something inappropriate was happening. She was to follow the plan accordingly so as to not backfire on her. It was risky, but she had no choice but to be willing to take her chances.

"And it happened in the middle of the night that the man was startled and bent forward; and behold, a woman was lying at his feet. So he said, 'Who are you?' And she answered, 'I am Ruth, your slave. Now spread your garment over your slave, for you are a redeemer.' Then he

said, 'May you be blessed of the LORD, my daughter. You have shown your last kindness to be better than the first, by not going after young men, whether poor or rich. So now, my daughter, do not fear. I will do for you whatever you say, for all my people in the city know that you are a woman of excellence. But now, although it is true that I am a redeemer, yet there is also a redeemer more closely related than I. Remain this night, and when morning comes, if he will redeem you, good; let him redeem you. But if he does not wish to redeem you, then I will redeem you, as the LORD lives. Lie down until morning.'"

So she lay at his feet until morning, and got up before one person could recognize another; and he said, 'Do not let it be known that the woman came to the threshing floor.' Again he said, 'Give me the shawl that is on you and hold it.' So she held it, and he measured six measures of barley and laid it on her. Then she went into the city" (NASB, Ruth 3: 8-15).

Boaz's reaction to Ruth was very positive. Naomi knew what she was doing when she advised her on what to do. Boaz did not misinterpret her intentions, but he commended her for being willing to follow the proper protocol and marry someone older when she could have been interested in younger men. As we discussed earlier, Ruth was beautiful, but her most attractive quality was her character. According to Boaz, everyone in the town knew of her "noble character." This might have been one of the reasons why Naomi waited a while before she advised Ruth to approach Boaz. People got to know and hear about her. There was no question about her intentions when she approached him.

"When she came to her mother-in-law, she said, 'How did it go, my daughter?' And she told her all that the man had done for her. She also said, 'These six measures of barley he gave to me, for he said, Do not go to your mother-in-law empty-handed.' Then she said, 'Wait, my

daughter, until you know how the matter turns out; for the man will not rest until he has settled it today'" (NASB, Ruth 3:16-18).

Naomi, once again, advised Ruth on the appropriate course of action. By now, she could tell Boaz's intentions by his actions. All they had to do was wait.

Life Lesson # 37:
Patiently Waiting vs. Passively Waiting

Sometimes, we feel like we are in a season of waiting; waiting to hear from a job offer, for a promotion, to "meet the one," or for God to show us the way forward. The tricky part of this type of season is to discern what we are supposed to be doing while we wait. Ruth and Naomi were not passively 'waiting on God.' Even as vulnerable widows, they took action by gleaning in the field and approaching Boaz at the appropriate time. They perfectly balanced 'human initiative' and 'God's intervention.' They acted in faith. They did what they could. They took a chance. They took advantage of every opportunity they were presented with, even if the chances were slim to none, and believed God could meet them there.

The key to a waiting or 'transition' period is knowing when to act and when to let go and wait and not confusing the two.

Psalm 40:1-3 (ESV) states:

> *"I waited patiently for the Lord;*
> *he inclined to me and heard my cry.*
> *He drew me up from the pit of destruction,*
> *out of the miry bog,*
> *and set my feet upon a rock,*
> *making my steps secure.*
> *He put a new song in my mouth,*

> *a song of praise to our God.*
> *Many will see and fear,*
> *and put their trust in the* Lord.*"*

The phrase "waited patiently" in the original Hebrew language was the one verb qāvâ, which meant to "wait," "wait for," "look for," "expect," and "hope."[38] The Strong's Concordance describes it as "the tension of enduring," "to look eagerly for," "to endure," "to remain."[39] There is action in the waiting. It's a resolution not to give up. The commitment to stay in position until we see what we desire comes to pass. It conveys a sense of perseverance. It goes beyond 'hoping' it comes to pass. It involves active faith and not a passive expectation.

Hebrews 6:13-15 (**ESV**) states:

> *"When God made his promise to Abraham, since there was no one greater for him to swear by, he swore by himself, saying, 'I will surely bless you and give you many descendants.' And so after waiting patiently, Abraham received what was promised."*

Once more, "waited patiently" shows up. This is often misinterpreted as "waiting passively," but is not what it means. The Greek word that is translated "patiently waited" or "patiently endured" is the verb makrothymeō, which means "longsuffering, to "not lose heart," "bear long," "suffer long," "patiently endure."[40] The Strongs dictionary defines it as "persevere patiently and bravely in enduring misfortunes and troubles."[41] Once more, the expression to "wait patiently" involves an active endurance during storms, trials, and uncertainties, which certainly will come as we step out in faith and obey God's assignment for us. We are meant to endure, do whatever God told us to do, and not give up until we see the promise come to pass. Galatians 6:9 states: *"And let us not grow weary of doing good, for in due season we will reap, if we do not give up."* Waiting patiently means walking confidently even when not seeing the harvest yet. It involves preparing the storehouse for the harvest and planning for it, even before it sprouts. We don't start pouting because it's not evident yet. We don't give up because it looks unlikely. We don't change our confession either. We press on in faith regardless of the circumstances. We speak faith, and we do not give up until it comes to fruition.

One aspect that we need to come to terms with is that there is always a purpose in the "waiting period." James 5:7-8 (NIV) states:

> *"Be patient, then, brothers and sisters, until the Lord's coming. See how the farmer waits for the land to yield its valuable crop, patiently waiting for the autumn and spring rains. You too, be patient and stand firm, because the Lord's coming is near."*

In our modern world, waiting might entail studying or going through training before attaining the job promotion we are looking for; we might need to gain experience in a specific area of ministry or a job before we are given the chance to serve where we really want to. Maybe we need to research and study God's Word about the specific area we are seeking victory. While we wait we can start confessing God's Word and His promises for that particular area too!

If God is not giving us what we desire yet, rest assured that it is not so that we suffer. The waiting period is part of the answer in

Patiently waiting does not mean passively waiting.

many instances. It's part of God's grace and providence to ensure we will be ready when the time comes. It's often also a test of our faith. If we can endure the waiting period, the Lord can trust us with His assignment. James 1:12 (NASB) states: *"Blessed is a man who perseveres under trial; for once he has been approved, he will receive the crown of life which the Lord has promised to those who love Him."* The key is to discern the purpose of this waiting time. If we are being tested, we should persevere and endure. If we are being trained, we should take advantage of that opportunity. If we are meant to be building the foundation of what we are hoping for, we should get to work. Patiently waiting does not mean passively waiting.

Personal Story: Waiting to Meet My Husband

When I was about 12 years old, I started praying for my future husband. My parents emphasized the importance of marrying the person God had for you, and I did not want to make a mistake in that area. I knew he had to be a Christian first and foremost. When I was 16 years old, the Lord spoke to my twin sister Ana and me about His plans to take us to the United States via a College Tennis Scholarship. We were playing tennis up until that point but weren't sure exactly what God's plans were yet. However, when we heard from the Lord in that area, our efforts became laser-focused on that specific goal. So much so that I was not interested in meeting anyone in Argentina. The Lord was taking me to the United States, so I assumed that was where my husband was.

Fast forward almost four years, and I moved to the United States for College by the grace of God. We were playing Tennis for Liberty University, one of the Largest Christian Universities in the World. The Lord was faithful! I was so excited to be there. It was everything I had dreamed of and more. I also had high hopes of meeting my future husband there. There were thousands of great-looking, intelligent, athletic, and talented Christian young guys. It was a 'no-brainer.' That's where I was going to meet my husband, or was it?

God had different plans for me. Even though I did meet some great guys, the Lord spoke to me clearly, and I knew that this was a season to study and focus on what He had placed in front of me and not to start dating yet. This might not be everyone's story, but it was what the Lord required from me, so I surrendered. I moved to another University in my Junior year, but that was not where my husband was either. Then I moved to Florida for a year and then to Louisiana for three years while I pursued an MBA, but that was not where my husband was either. After almost 8 years of living in the US, the Lord started speaking to me and placing in my heart that my husband was in Florida, where I was planning on moving after graduation.

Once I finally moved to Florida and got a job, I knew this was finally the season to meet my future husband. And God was faithful. We met on a Christian dating site first and then at the Tennis Courts in Delray Beach. It's a long story, but we've been married for over 11 years, have 3 wonderful children and I must say that it was worth the wait! It was not always easy to wait and listen to that "still small voice" that told me to trust Him, in fact I did not always listened right away! I did not get it right every time, but the Lord was gracious and faithful.

The waiting period was difficult, but it was necessary. The Lord had me waiting in that one area of my life, but He gave me plenty of great blessings in other areas, like friendships, opportunities to serve Him, travel, study and grow. Ideally, I should have embraced those moments without worrying about what was next, but this was not always the case. I often feared that God had completely forgotten about me in this area. Many times I would feel lonely, but that helped me draw closer to God and He would often bring friendships and some amazing people into my life. I was never alone. This season was a season of preparation; looking back, I am so glad I did not rush it.

A significant lesson to take from this is also not to look at other people's "timings" and compare our lives with theirs. It was easy to look at those friends who married right after college and get discouraged or frustrated. It's also important to not doubt if we believe we heard from God in a specific area. If we need confirmation, we can ask him again, but it's never a good idea to dwell on those feelings and doubts. John 10:27 (ESV) states: *"My sheep hear my voice, and I know them, and they follow me."* Remember, you have the ability to hear directly from God. Do that, and do not pay attention to any other 'voices.' If the Lord is making you wait, trust him. He has not forgotten about you.

Ruth was gleaning in the fields, working hard, and providing for her mother-in-law when the Lord brought Boaz into her life. She had demonstrated character, bravery, loyalty, and hard work, all qualities that Boaz could not ignore. It was not just her beauty that attracted him to her. She could have returned to Moab and felt sorry for herself. Instead, she took a risk. The Bible did not mention Orpah again, but Ruth was assigned an entire Old Testament book to share with the world for eternity. What we choose to do in the waiting period matters. Even seemingly "small" steps of obedience and faith will bring a large harvest.

Psalm 66: 8-12 (**NASB**) states:

"Bless our God, you peoples,
And sound His praise abroad,
Who keeps us in life,
And does not allow our feet to slip.
For You have put us to the test, God;
You have refined us as silver is refined.
You brought us into the net;
You laid an oppressive burden upon us.
You made men ride over our heads;
We went through fire and through water.
Yet You brought us out into a place of abundance."

Let's persevere amid trials and uncertainty and endure with faith, and we will be able to experience God's abundant blessings in our lives.

Questions to Consider

What promises am I still waiting for God to fulfill in my life?

_____

_____

_____

Do I tend to follow my emotions when times get tough, or do I hold on to the Word of God to keep me stable during the wait?

_____

_____

_____

Breakthrough Prayer

Dear Lord, help me have an active faith and the expectation that You can give me my breakthrough today. On the other hand, if there is a necessary "waiting period," help me discern the purpose behind it and use that time wisely, not giving up, but working hard in whatever it is that You give me to do. Help me to rely on your Word and not on my feelings when things get tough. Forgive me if I have doubted or turned away from your purposes. I cast out every spirit of doubt, discouragement, loneliness, and double-mindedness from my life, and I declare that I will endure this trial. I will see your promises come to fruition in my life. I will not give up when times get tough. I have the victory in Jesus' name. Amen.

Day Thirty-eight

The Decision That Changed Everything
(Ruth 4:1-12)

"Now Boaz went up to the gate and sat down there, and behold, the redeemer of whom Boaz spoke was passing by, so he said, 'Come over here, friend, sit down here.' And he came over and sat down" (NASB, Ruth 4:1).

Boaz intended to marry Ruth, but he first had to ensure he was legally allowed to. Marriage in ancient Israel was very different from today. Several laws, regulations, and protocols had to be followed, especially in the case of Ruth. These laws were in place to protect the most vulnerable. One of the laws stated that the land that Elimelech had abandoned or sold when he left for Moab could only be purchased back by a relative. However, there was an order that a relative could purchase. Boaz had to make sure his friend, who was first in line to "redeem" or "re-purchase" the land, had no interest in exercising that right:

"Then he took ten men of the elders of the city and said, 'Sit down here.' So they sat down. And he said to the redeemer, 'Naomi, who has returned from the land of Moab, has to sell the plot of land which belonged to our brother Elimelech. So I thought that I would inform you, saying, 'Buy it before those who are sitting here, and before the elders of my people. If you will redeem it, redeem it; but if not, tell me so that

I may know; for there is no one except you to redeem it, and I am after you.' And he said, 'I will redeem it'" (NASB, Ruth 4:2-4).

The opportunity to purchase land was considered a privilege. The land was not traded in the "open market" but kept within the family. This seemed like a great prospect to his friend, and he wanted to jump on it right away. However, this "land deal" came with a catch. Boaz went on to explain that if he agreed to purchase the land, he would also be agreeing to marry the widowed daughter-in-law of Elimelech:

"Then Boaz said, 'On the day you buy the field from the hand of Naomi, you must also acquire Ruth the Moabitess, the widow of the deceased, in order to raise up the name of the deceased on his inheritance.' Then the redeemer said, 'I cannot redeem it for myself, otherwise I would jeopardize my own inheritance. Redeem it for yourself; you may have my right of redemption, since I cannot redeem it'" (NASB, Ruth 4: 5-6).

According to this translation, the "guardian-redeemer" friend of Boaz declined the "deal" right away when he heard the terms because it would legally affect his estate. This could be a logical interpretation. However, there are differing views on the translation of these last few sentences, and it is also likely that Boaz did not tell him that he would have to marry Ruth but that he announced that he intended to marry Ruth, the widowed daughter-in-law of the previous land-owner. If this were the case, the response would make more sense because regardless of the purchase of the land, if Ruth and Boaz ever had a son, he would inherit the rights of the land, "endangering" his purchase.

Regardless of the exact negotiations, the decline of the offer was great news for Boaz. He was now legally allowed to marry Ruth. This was a game-changer for everyone! Boaz, Ruth, and Naomi.

Naomi had legal protection and was also now co-owner of the land. This decision changed everything:

> *"Now this was the custom in former times in Israel concerning the redemption and the exchange of land to confirm any matter: a man removed his sandal and gave it to another; and this was the way of confirmation in Israel. So the redeemer said to Boaz, 'Buy it for yourself.' And he removed his sandal. Then Boaz said to the elders and all the people, 'You are witnesses today that I have bought from the hand of Naomi all that belonged to Elimelech and all that belonged to Chilion and Mahlon. Furthermore, I have acquired Ruth the Moabitess, the widow of Mahlon, to be my wife in order to raise up the name of the deceased on his inheritance, so that the name of the deceased will not be eliminated from his brothers or from the court of his birth place; you are witnesses today.' And all the people who were in the court, and the elders, said, 'We are witnesses. May the LORD make the woman who is coming into your home like Rachel and Leah, both of whom built the house of Israel; and may you achieve wealth in Ephrathah and become famous in Bethlehem. Moreover, may your house be like the house of Perez whom Tamar bore to Judah, through the descendants whom the LORD will give you by this young woman'"* (NASB, Ruth 4:7-12).

This was a day of freedom for Ruth and Naomi and a day of joy for Ruth and Boaz.

LIFE LESSON #38:
THE VALUE OF "SPOKEN BLESSINGS"

As you may have noticed, the elders pronounced a special blessing over Boaz and Ruth. They blessed her with fertility, strong descendants who would build the family of Israel, and offspring like that of Perez, an ancestor of the house of Judah.[42] These blessings were not just formalities; they carried weight. As we will find out soon, they all came to pass.

Blessings are considered "a conduit for spiritual and physical potential" in the Jewish culture. "God blessed Adam and Eve to fill the world, Abraham was called a blessing for all his descendants, Jacob stole the first-born blessing and altered his future, and the high priests blessed the nation with an ever-expanding relationship with peace," [43] to name a few. In fact, the Old Testament is filled with "spoken blessings" that were fulfilled. In today's Christian culture this concept is often referred to as "faith confession" or the "power of your words." In the book of Hebrews in the New Testament we find these uttered blessings described as "invoking blessings by faith": *"By faith, Isaac invoked future blessings on Jacob and Esau"* (ESV, Hebrews 11:20). Earlier, the apostle Paul had explained how God's words were received by Abraham by faith:

> *"For when God made the promise to Abraham, since He could swear an oath by no one greater, He swore by Himself, saying, 'indeed I will greatly bless you and I will greatly multiply you.' And so, having patiently waited, he obtained the promise"* (NASB, Hebrews 6:13-15).

Spoken blessings were approached with reverence and held at face value. Hopefully, we can come to a greater appreciation of the power that lies not only in our words but also, most importantly, in the blessings that God has already pronounced over us throughout the Scriptures. Hebrews 4:12 (NASB) states:

> *"For the word of God is living and active, and sharper than any two-edged sword, even penetrating as far as the division of soul and spirit, of both joints and marrow, and able to judge the thoughts and intentions of the heart."*

They are not mere "wishes" and "hopes." They are to be taken as fact. Once God commands something, His words have ultimate authority. His words carry the power to create that reality and bring it to pass in our lives.

Isaiah 55:10-11 (**NASB**) states:

> *"For as the rain and the snow come down from heaven,*
> *And do not return there without watering the earth*
> *And making it produce and sprout,*
> *And providing seed to the sower and bread to the eater;*
> *So will My word be which goes out of My mouth;*
> *It will not return to Me empty,*
> *Without accomplishing what I desire,*
> *And without succeeding in the purpose for which I sent it."*

When God pronounces blessings over us through His Word, He not only means it, but they carry the power to create that reality. We must choose to believe that and receive those blessings by faith in order for them to be manifested. We are also called to speak those words. Romans 10:10 (ESV) states: *"For with the heart one believes and is justified, and with the mouth one confesses and is saved."* This is not a common practice in our culture today, but the value of it is all over the Scriptures. If we ignore these principles, we are choosing to miss out on the unlimited power that can be tapped into through the power of speaking the truth of God out loud. We can create a new reality by believing what God promised us in His Word and confessing it in faith.

Personal Story:
Calling Things That Are Not as If They Were

When my twin sister and I were 12, my dad joined a 'multilevel marketing business' based in the United States. One of the characteristics of this unique 'business model' was the motivational books and tapes they made available to those who signed up. The idea was to change your way of thinking by filling your mind and heart with these inspirational messages and success stories, so that you would stay the course. Many of them were Christian leadership books and were instrumental in changing our lives. We learned about dreaming big, goal setting, having a positive outlook in life and, yes, "the power of the spoken word."

One of the big changes we made due to one of these books was to pick one sport out of a few we practiced and finally 'stick to it.' We prayed about it, and we then decided that tennis would be it. The only issue was that we were 12 years old already and not any good. Most of our peers had started way earlier than we had. Regardless of that disadvantage, we put in all of our efforts and worked twice as hard as most kids our age to make up for it.

Something else we did, which I remember vividly, is changing our "confessions" or "affirmations." I remember writing down statements such as "I played for the best universities in the world" (which many years later came to pass). At one point, my sister and I wrote with chalk on the tennis wall of our country club, "Tucuman '96," which was our one-year goal from that point in time. Tucuman was a province in our home country in Argentina, and it referred to a yearly trip that our tennis club held. Only the best players were invited to be a part of it. They would get special matching outfits and get on a bus for about 12 hours, stay at players' homes in San Miguel de Tucuman in Argentina, and play a tournament there. This was our dream, and it seemed impossible because we had just started taking this sport seriously. We looked at those words written with chalk daily as we practiced against the wall, and we also started speaking them out loud, saying "ganare Tucuman '96," which meant "I will win Tucuman '96" over and over again. Not only were we invited to that tournament less than a year later, but a few years later, we both received the Annual Award in our Club for the players with the Most Progress and eventually Full Scholarships to play tennis in one of the largest NCAA Division 1 Private Christian Universities in the World.

The story is a lot longer, and the examples of speaking what we desired are countless, but I want to encourage you to do it because it not only works, but that is the way God himself creates things out of nothing. Romans 4:17b (ESV) states that God *"calls into existence the things that do not exist."* Proverbs 18:21 (ESV) states: *"Death and life are in the power of the tongue, and those who love it will eat its fruits."* There is power in the words we speak to bring forth a new reality into our lives. If these words are based on God's Holy Word and His promises for us, they are even more powerful because they carry His authority. They must produce fruit.

As foreign as this concept might seem, it's practiced all over the Bible and even nowadays in the Christian and even the secular world! Let's align our words with God's truth and speak His promises for us, and we will witness its benefits in our lives.

Questions to Consider

Do I choose to believe what God says and accept it as the ultimate truth?

_____

_____

_____

Am I willing to transform my reality by replacing my words with God's promises for me?

_____

_____

_____

Am I willing to walk in the reality of God's promises by faith, even before I see it come to pass?

_____

_____

_____

Breakthrough Prayer

Thank you, Lord, for your beautiful promises You have already spoken over me and my family. I receive every blessing by faith, and I choose the reality of your Word over the deceit of my thoughts and emotions. Please help me get to know You and your word so intimately that my words are replaced with your life-giving words. Thank You for a new beginning. Thank You for a beautiful new season of life that is starting to sprout. I give You all the glory. In Jesus' name. Amen.

Day Thirty-nine

The Ultimate Miracle (Ruth 4:13-22)

"So Boaz took Ruth, and she became his wife, and he had relations with her. And the Lord enabled her to conceive, and she gave birth to a son" (NASB, Ruth 4:13).

This is the happy ending that only God can create. He not only provided a husband and redeemer to a foreign widow who had no hope, but now He allowed her to give birth to a son after being barren for over 10 years. Not only that, but her son Obed became the grandfather of King David and was part of the lineage of the promised Messiah, Jesus Christ. That divinely appointed marriage was not just a blessing to Ruth and Boaz; it became a legacy of faith for eternity.

After the beautiful news, Naomi took center stage. The women who had witnessed her humble return to Bethlehem were now praising her and recognizing God's hand of blessing over her. She had been blessed with a daughter-in-law who was more valuable than "seven sons," a guardian-redeemer, and a grandson conceived by a miracle of God:

"Then the women said to Naomi, 'Blessed is the Lord who has not left you without a redeemer today, and may his name become famous in Israel. May he also be to you one who restores life and sustains your old age; for your daughter-in-law, who loves you and is better to you than seven sons, has given birth to him'" (NASB, Ruth 4:14-15).

The child was a blessing to Naomi as much as to Ruth. He was a symbolic son to Naomi, recognized as such by Jewish law, and the one responsible for her in her old age. Her life had been restored and was evidence of God's goodness and power. Every hardship and negative event in her past had been replaced by a blessing.

Here is another example of the "spoken blessing," where the woman uttered a blessing regarding the child's destiny, Obed, saying that he "May become famous throughout Israel!"

For the two "sons" that Naomi lost, she gained a grandson and a daughter-in-law that was "better to her than seven sons."

> *"Then Naomi took the child and laid him in her lap, and became his nurse. And the neighbor women gave him a name, saying, 'A son has been born to Naomi!' So they named him Obed. He is the father of Jesse, the father of David"* (NASB, Ruth 4: 16-17).

Naomi became her grandchild's (Obed) caregiver, bringing new purpose and joy to her life. She was also able to move in with Boaz and Ruth. She had a wonderful family and a great calling, as she helped raise King David's grandfather. The boy was, according to Jewish Law, also considered Naomi's son and thus a descendant of Elimelek:

The Lineage of King David

> *"Now these are the generations of Perez: Perez fathered Hezron, Hezron fathered Ram, and Ram fathered Amminadab, and Amminadab fathered Nahshon, and Nahshon fathered Salmon, and Salmon fathered Boaz, and Boaz fathered Obed, and Obed fathered Jesse, and Jesse fathered David"* (NASB, Ruth 4:18-22).

The Lord restored Naomi. He gave her a new family, restored her "family property" through Boaz, and gave her a grandson, Obed, whom she had the privilege of caring for and who would eventually take care of her in her old age. Ruth became the great-grandmother of King David, and Naomi his great-great-grandmother. Then, the family tree continued, leading all the way to the birth of the promised Jewish Savior and Messiah, Jesus Christ of Nazareth (Matthew 1:1-17).

Life Lesson #39:
We Were Created with an Eternal Purpose

Obed was born by a miracle of God. A miraculous conception was usually a sign that the son had a special assignment or call of God. Sarah, Rebecca, and Rachel were all examples in which God had to intervened for them to be able to conceive and their children ended up having a heavenly destiny in their lives.[44] Likewise, when we are "born-again" by the Spirit of God (John 3:3), this is a supernatural event that God brings to pass through our faith. We are then supernaturally conceived as a brand-new creation, a person called forth by God to fulfill a divine calling in this world. 2 Corinthians 5:16-20a (ESV) explains this mystery:

> *"From now on, therefore, we regard no one according to the flesh. Even though we once regarded Christ according to the flesh, we regard him thus no longer. Therefore, if anyone is in Christ, he is a new creation. The old has passed away; behold, the new has come. All this is from God, who through Christ reconciled us to himself and gave us the ministry of reconciliation; that is, in Christ God was reconciling the world to himself, not counting their trespasses against them, and entrusting to us the message of reconciliation. Therefore, we are ambassadors for Christ..."*

God can take a person in the most hopeless and tragic situation and turn his/her life into an eternal legacy. He has done it before and wants to do it again in your life today. He is not looking for perfect people with a spotless journey or an impressive resume. He is looking for people who believe in Him and choose His path above their own.

Questions to Consider

Am I willing to leave behind my old life and identity and embrace the life of purpose and legacy God has in store for me?

_____

_____

_____

Breakthrough Prayer

Thank you, Lord, for saving and loving me and calling me to live a life of purpose and meaning. I believe what You say about me, not what the world thinks of me. Thank You for making me a unique work of art. I embrace this new identity in Your Word and refuse to return to my old ways. I am excited about the new life You have custom-designed for me to walk in. Thank You that You will lead me and protect me at every turn. I don't have to be afraid. I place my trust in You. My life is yours. In Jesus' name. Amen.

Day Forty

Main Takeaways from the Life of Ruth

Thank you for embarking on this profound journey through Ruth's life! The Life Lessons we gathered from this captivating Biblical account underline the threat of rash decisions, particularly in times of crisis. They also emphasize the importance of seeking the Lord's counsel before we embark on any journey, regardless of its magnitude. Just as a well-trained pilot can remain calm in a turbulent flight, making wise decisions to lead his passengers to a safe landing, God isn't caught off guard by our circumstances, and He can steer our lives when they seem to be heading in the wrong direction. If we allow Him to lead us, He will take us to a victorious landing at the end of our lives!

We have also learned that God should always be our foremost priority, irrespective of how busy we get. This is the key to victory in every domain of life. Every aspect of life is interconnected. We cannot compartmentalize God.

Our study revealed that the Lord is deeply concerned for the oppressed and the overlooked. He can turn the most daunting circumstances into a testament to His grace. His ability to create anew is unmatched, and our past should never dictate our future! When we trust Him, He blots out our past transgressions and the shame of our youth, painting a fresh, vibrant picture of our lives. He makes all things new!

Furthermore, we discovered that God's expectations of us are not rooted in perfection but in our willingness to heed His voice. It is far more beneficial to take action with the intention of obeying Him, even if we are not 100% certain than to be paralyzed by the fear of making a misstep. He understands our human nature and has made provisions for our inevitable mistakes!

Another profound insight we've gained is God's limitless goodness. He not only answers our prayers but His blessings overflow and surpass our expectations. His blessings are not one-dimensional either; they permeate every aspect of our lives, communities, and even future generations. They are not confined to the specific needs they meet. They are all-encompassing and a testament to His infinite wisdom, knowledge, power, and generosity!

Finally, we learned to sow seeds with our words by speaking God's promises over our circumstances. The harvest is not always instant, and there are things we need to do while we wait. Discerning what those actions are in the waiting period is critical to reaping all the blessings God has in store.

In conclusion, the story of Ruth gives us a great illustration of how God can and wants to help those who suffer and is more than able to not only help them in their struggles but also take a life that seemed hopeless and turn it into a legacy of faith that transcends time and place. There is no life that is too far gone for God to redeem. No person is too insignificant in His eyes. He created you and values your life immensely! He sees you and wants your life to be a one-of-a-kind work of art that blesses those around you and the generations to come! Will you heed His call today? He will not disappoint you!

Questions to Consider

Which part of Ruth or Naomi's lives resonated with me the most?

_____

_____

_____

What did I learn from this story that can apply to my own life today?

_____

_____

_____

My Prayer Over You

Dear Lord, I thank You for those who have been faithful in going over this 40-day journey alongside me. I pray that Your Word will not return void but that it will accomplish the purpose for which it was sent. I also pray this study has helped them gain a deeper appreciation for Your Word and a greater understanding of who You are and what You can do with those who are willing to surrender their lives to You. I also pray that if they do not know You, they will trust Jesus as their Lord and Savior and receive the Baptism of the Holy Spirit and the grace to live a victorious, Christ-centered life, filled with purpose and fruit. I bless their journey of faith, relationships, careers, decisions, health, and emotional lives. I pray that you will turn any seemingly impossible situation in their lives around for their good right now, in Jesus' name! I pray for breakthroughs in every area of their lives, freedom, abundant joy, and good news from now on! I declare them free from any oppression, fear, deception, addiction, or any chains that might be keeping them in bondage. I declare them healed from any infirmities, heartache, trauma, or anything hindering them from living the life you have planned for them. Your Word states in John 8:36 (ESV) that … *"if the Son sets you free, you will be free indeed,"* so we receive that freedom and victory right now by faith! Thank You for hearing our prayers. Thank You for loving us so infinitely. In Jesus' name, we pray. Amen.

Conclusion

It's been a long and hopefully fruitful and rewarding Journey. We looked at distinct people with diverse situations, but they all desperately needed God. From a wealthy housewife who was shunned from everyday life because of her physical limitations, a prophet who could not follow God's assignment because of his deeply ingrained views of the people he was called to minister to, and a homeless foreigner widow with no rights in society who was happy to have the lowest of jobs to survive. They were all prisoners of their circumstances, and if it weren't for God's divine interventions, their lives would have ended in disgrace and likely greater misfortune.

The Power of a Desperate Situation

One of the profound realizations I've had recently is the fact that going through a desperate situation has the potential to catapult us to a level of freedom that we have never experienced before! How would that happen? Well, if we choose to surrender our situation and cry out to God for help, sincerely and from the depths of our souls, He begins a work in our hearts that otherwise, we would have missed. That genuine brokenness before him allows for some of those strongholds that have been holding us back to finally break off! They might have been in the form of pride, entitlement, self-pity, people-pleasing, our version of the truth, or even issues like addiction, and the list continues. At a point of real crisis, we are finally open to the truth and willing to let go of the excuses and the barriers we had all along. We are also open to questioning how we made decisions and even led our lives up until that moment.

When we finally hand it all to God, the good, the bad, and the ugly, we suddenly become free to see possibilities that we did not see before. We are willing to do things that we never dared before. We become eager to dream again and move forward. Because, at that point in time, we have nothing to lose and everything to gain. When we give our desperate situation, along with our hearts, to God, we begin to change, and as a result, our life takes a significant turn for the better. And this is only the beginning.

We may have thought we were at a disadvantage in this hardship, but the truth is that we now have a huge advantage! We can use this crisis to let God take over and turn our lives around! That is our most important victory. Everything will change because we were changed, and we are no longer walking this life alone!

The Most Desperate Moment Anyone Could Face

Before I wrap up this book, I want to discuss the "elephant in the room." As desperate as our earthly situation could be, God is able to intervene and turn everything around for our good, even when it was our own fault to begin with! Nothing is impossible to God!

However, there is one situation in which, if we fall into it, there is no going back. It would become eternally too late to cry out to God. It could not be reversed. When Jesus was on earth, He told a story that illustrates this Desperate Situation. He shared it as a warning:

> *"Now there was a rich man, and he habitually dressed in purple and fine linen, enjoying himself in splendor every day. And a poor man named Lazarus was laid at his gate, covered with sores, and longing to be fed from the scraps which fell from the rich man's table; not only that, the dogs also were coming and licking his sores. Now it happened that the poor man died and was carried away by the angels to Abraham's arms; and the rich man also died and was buried. And in Hades he raised*

his eyes, being in torment, and saw Abraham far away and Lazarus in his arms. And he cried out and said, 'Father Abraham, have mercy on me and send Lazarus, so that he may dip the tip of his finger in water and cool off my tongue, for I am in agony in this flame.' But Abraham said, 'Child, remember that during your life you received your good things, and likewise Lazarus bad things; but now he is being comforted here, and you are in agony. And besides all this, between us and you a great chasm has been set, so that those who want to go over from here to you will not be able, nor will any people cross over from there to us.' And he said, 'Then I request of you, father, that you send him to my father's house— for I have five brothers—in order that he may warn them, so that they will not come to this place of torment as well.' But Abraham said, 'They have Moses and the Prophets; let them hear them.' But he said, 'No, father Abraham, but if someone goes to them from the dead, they will repent!' But he said to him, 'If they do not listen to Moses and the Prophets, they will not be persuaded even if someone rises from the dead'" (NASB, Luke 16:19-31).

Just like this story reveals, if we die without Christ, there is no going back. It would be too late to repent. It would be too late to have faith in Jesus. There are no second chances after we die. Today is your opportunity to make the most important decision of your life. If you have never decided to follow God before, today is your day! The Bible states that *"for all have sinned and fall short of the glory of God"* (ESV, Romans 3:23), which means that everyone, with no distinction, has been separated from God because of sin. The Bible also states in Romans 6:23 (ESV) that *"For the wages of sin is death, but the free gift of God is eternal life in Christ Jesus our Lord."* This means that we all deserve to die and go to hell, each one of us. Nobody deserves to go to Heaven; nobody is good enough for that.

However, there is a free gift available to those who believe in God, and that gift is eternal life, which encompasses not only going to Heaven when we die but having a relationship with God and a blessed life while on earth too! John 3:16-18 (NASB) states:

> *"For God so loved the world, that He gave His only Son, so that everyone who believes in Him will not perish, but have eternal life. For God did not send the Son into the world to judge the world, but so that the world might be saved through Him. The one who believes in Him is not judged; the one who does not believe has been judged already, because he has not believed in the name of the only Son of God."*

This passage tells us that those who do not believe are already condemned. God does not send people to hell; they go there because that is where sinners end up by default. There is no reversal. Once you are there, it is too late to repent!

The good news is that you are on this side of eternity today. If you are reading this, no matter where you are, your heart is pumping, you have air in your lungs and can make the choice to believe in God and follow Him! When Jesus was hanging on the cross, two criminals were hanging at each side of him. One mocked him, but the other one asked for mercy:

> *"One of the criminals who were hanged there was hurling abuse at Him, saying, 'Are You not the Christ? Save Yourself and us!' But the other responded, and rebuking him, said, 'Do you not even fear God, since you are under the same sentence of condemnation? And we indeed are suffering justly, for we are receiving what we deserve for our crimes; but this man has done nothing wrong.' And he was saying, 'Jesus, remember me when You come into Your kingdom!' And He said to him, 'Truly I say to you, today you will be with Me in Paradise'"* (NASB, Luke 23:39-43).

I love this story because it describes the simplicity of the faith needed to go to Heaven. No sin is too great for God to forgive, and it's not too late as long as we are still on this side of eternity!

The Bible states in Romans 10:9 (ESV), *"If you confess with your mouth that Jesus is Lord and believe in your heart that God raised him from the dead, you will be saved."* It's as simple as that. Jesus did all the work by dying on the cross for us; our job is to believe!

It's not about what words we use, when, or where we are located when we believe. We can make a decision for Christ on our deathbed, in a prison cell, while driving in a car, alone, or in a church full of people. It doesn't make a difference to God. He sees our hearts, and that is enough! That being said, I have provided a sample prayer of salvation (or rededication for those who maybe believed in the past but have not been walking close to God). You can follow this prayer or use your own words. Remember it's not the prayer that saves you, but the fact that you are placing your trust in Jesus and His Sacrifice on the cross for your salvation. Ephesians 2:8-9 (NIV) states, *"For it is by grace you have been saved, through faith—and this is not from yourselves, it is the gift of God— not by works, so that no one can boast."*

You don't need to wait another moment. 2 Corinthians 6:2 states *"now is the favorable time; behold, now is the day of salvation."*

Salvation/Rededication Prayer

Thank you, God, for sending Your Son, Jesus Christ, to live a sinless life and die on the cross in my place. Thank You that He rose from the dead on the third day and made a way for me to be saved! I believe in Him and accept Him as my savior and the Lord of my life. Forgive me of my sin, wash, heal, and set me free from any darkness, oppression, bondage, addiction, sickness, or any work of the enemy. I am Yours. Make me a vessel for your glory. Help me live for You every day of my life. Thank You for Your salvation! In Jesus' name. Amen!

Welcome to the Family of God!

If You prayed this prayer, congratulations! You just made the most important decision of your life, and You will not regret it! The Bible tells us that in John 1:12-13 (ESV) that:

> *"But to all who did receive him, who believed in his name, he gave the right to become children of God, who were born, not of blood nor of the will of the flesh nor of the will of man, but of God."*

Welcome to the family of God!

The Power to Live a Life of Victory

Whether you have been a believer for a long time or just received Jesus for the first time today, the Bible teaches something crucial: we need to be empowered to live the life God intended for us to live here on earth and fulfill His purpose. Unfortunately, most believers do not get past the salvation prayer and miss out on the most incredible blessing here on earth: the empowerment of the Holy Spirit. Without this empowerment, it would be virtually impossible to follow most life lessons in the Word of God!

Romans 8:14-15 (ESV) states:

> *"For all who are led by the Spirit of God are sons of God. For you did not receive the spirit of slavery to fall back into fear, but you have received the Spirit of adoption as sons, by whom we cry, 'Abba! Father!'"*

Some of the proofs that we are indeed children of God are: the fruit in our life and our ability to be led by the Spirit. Unfortunately, many people try to accomplish this fruit on their own, and they get frustrated! We cannot walk the way God wants us to without being baptized by the Holy Spirit. John the Baptist explained this requirement in Matthew 3:11 (ESV) when he told his followers:

"I baptize you with water for repentance, but he who is coming after me is mightier than I, whose sandals I am not worthy to carry. He will baptize you with the Holy Spirit and fire."

Before Jesus left this earth, after He appeared to more than 500 witnesses (1 Corinthians 15:3-8) and spent at least 40 days with the disciples, he commanded them to wait and not get to work in the ministry until they received the "Baptism of the Holy Spirit." Acts 1:3-5 (NASB) states:

"To these He also presented Himself alive after His suffering, by many convincing proofs, appearing to them over a period of forty days and speaking of things regarding the kingdom of God. Gathering them together, He commanded them not to leave Jerusalem, but to wait for what the Father had promised, 'Which,' He said, 'you heard of from Me; for John baptized with water, but you will be baptized with the Holy Spirit not many days from now.'"

In John 14:15-17 (ESV) Jesus said:

"If you love me, you will keep my commandments. And I will ask the Father, and he will give you another Helper, to be with you forever, even the Spirit of truth, whom the world cannot receive, because it neither sees him nor knows him. You know him, for he dwells with you and will be in you."

And in verse 26 he continues by saying:

"But the Helper, the Holy Spirit, whom the Father will send in my name, he will teach you all things and bring to your remembrance all that I have said to you."

In Acts 19:1-7 (NASB) there is an instance in which Paul made it explicit that there are two kinds of Baptisms, one in water and one in the Holy Spirit:

"Now it happened that while Apollos was in Corinth, Paul passed through the upper country and came to Ephesus, and found some disciples. He said to them, 'Did you receive the Holy Spirit when you believed?' And they said to him, 'On the contrary, we have not even heard if there is a Holy Spirit.' And he said, 'Into what then were you baptized?' And they said, 'Into John's Baptism.' Paul said, 'John baptized with a Baptism of repentance, telling the people to believe in Him who was coming after him, that is, in Jesus.' When they heard this, they were baptized in the name of the Lord Jesus. And when Paul had laid hands upon them, the Holy Spirit came on them and they began speaking with tongues and prophesying. There were about twelve men in all."

In Acts 11 Peter was recounting an experience he had when he was speaking to some men about the Lord, and they received the Baptism of the Holy Spirit; they were not disciples; they were just regular gentile men, and the Spirit told him to "make no distinction" (v.12) when it came to what type of men they were:

"As I began to speak, the Holy Spirit fell on them just as on us at the beginning. And I remembered the word of the Lord, how he said, 'John baptized with water, but you will be baptized with the Holy Spirit'" (ESV, Acts 11:15-16).

I'm sharing these Bible verses as proof that this is crucial and necessary for those who believe in Jesus. It's not an option if you want to be led by The Holy Spirit, and as we just read in Acts 19:1-7, it is possible to be saved and not be baptized by the Holy Spirit. These are two different things.

That being said, although it is possible to receive the Baptism of the Holy Spirit at home while praying, I have found out that people are much more likely to receive it when someone who has been Baptized by the Holy Spirit and is anointed, prays for and lays hands on them for that very purpose. Unfortunately, that is not as common as it should be. If you want to receive the Baptism of the Holy Spirit, I pray that the Lord will lead you to the right place where He is allowed to move and His power and anointing are ready to be poured out! You will not regret it!

Personal Story:
The Baptism of the Holy Spirit When I was 15

I grew up in a Christian home, got saved at the age of 3, and went to a Baptist Church every Sunday with my parents. They both served God. I believed in God, and I even remember reading the "Bible in One Year" at the age of 12, wanting to know more but not genuinely understanding much of what it said. I was also pretty shy about my faith and during worship.

When I was 15 years old, a lady from our church told my twin sister and me about a summer camp from a different denomination, and we decided to go. Up until that point, we had faith, but something was lacking that we did not know was available to us as believers.

After that summer camp, our lives were changed forever. We experienced the presence of God like never before. I remember the worship service going all night one time. The presence of God was so strong that nobody wanted to leave. We would worship and dance along with all the other teenagers. I remember this particular morning going to bed after worshipping all night, feeling like Jesus was right there next to me. I felt so much peace and joy, like sleeping on a cloud. I woke up the following day, and all I wanted to do was pray and spend time with God. I wanted to tell everyone about Jesus. I wanted to worship and read the Bible. That's all I wanted to do. I did not know what had happened to me, but it was the best feeling in the world. God's strong presence in my life continued for several years after that. It would dwindle at times, but it never went off completely.

Until then, I had been shy and kept my faith to myself. But ever since that day, I have become bold. I started sharing the gospel with strangers; I worshipped and raised my hands in church. I started understanding what I read in the Bible and hearing the Holy Spirit lead me in my everyday life. My prayer life went to the next level, and my life was never the same!

I remember going back to my Baptist church and not understanding why everyone looked so "dead." Why weren't they on fire for God like we were? Why was their worship so "mechanical?" Why weren't they singing louder, raising their hands, dancing, or showing any enthusiasm for what they were singing? They could not see or feel what we felt; it was that simple. But why? What was the reason?

My sister and I did not understand where the difference was. We then met a young guy named Cesar at a youth group who had experienced the same thing we had and could explain what it was. He said that we had experienced the "Baptism of the Holy Spirit" and that some churches, like our Baptist church, do not always believe in it or emphasize it.

It took me years to fully grasp why some people understood the need for this Baptism and why some people were so against it. It did not make any sense. This was a game-changer in my Christian walk; why would people be afraid of it?

The reality is that, unfortunately, some churches have misrepresented what it is. Maybe out of ignorance. Some people have been led by emotions and blamed the Holy Spirit for it, so they gave Him a bad reputation. Regardless of what others have done, we cannot let fear of the unknown, pride, or ignorance keep us from the most incredible gift (after salvation) we could ever receive. The God of the Universe activated inside us to live a victorious Christian life; it doesn't get much better than that!

God will not force it on you. You need to be hungry and want it. Ask Him, and you will receive it! Luke 11: 9-13 (NASB) states:

"So I say to you, ask, and it will be given to you; seek, and you will find; [c]knock, and it will be opened to you. For everyone who asks receives, and the one who seeks finds, and to the one who knocks, it will be opened. Now which one of you fathers will his son ask for a fish, and instead of a fish, he will give him a snake? Or he will even ask for an egg, and his father will give him a scorpion? So if you, despite being evil, know how to give good gifts to your children, how much more will your heavenly Father give the Holy Spirit to those who ask Him?"

The difference between being Baptized in the Holy Spirit and not being Baptized in Him is tangible. Don't miss out!

Baptism of the Holy Spirit Prayer

Dear Lord Jesus, thank You for this journey. I pray You will reveal your truth and use my life for Your glory. If I have not been Baptized by the Holy Spirit yet, I pray that You do so today. If I have, give me a fresh touch, a renewal of your power, and anointing to live a Victorious Christian life. I pray that You open my eyes to see the spiritual side of life and have a hunger and thirst for You like never before! Give me the power to live in victory, discern between the truth and lies, and continue to grow in my faith through prayer, reading the Word, serving, and having regular fellowship with other believers. Burn everything that is not from You, and help me have a passion for you and your Kingdom. I thank you for your victory and your breakthrough in my life. In Jesus' name, I pray. Amen.

End Notes

Chapter 1: Hannah

1. Ebeling, Jennie R. *Women's Lives in Biblical Times*. Bloomsbury Academic & Professional, 2010, 14.
2. Ibid.
3. Hamilton, Mark W. "Review of Dietrich, Walter, the early monarchy in Israel: The tenth century B.C.E. (trans. Joachim Vette; biblical encyclopedia 3; Leiden/Boston: Brill, 2007)." *The Journal of Hebrew Scriptures*, vol. 10, 31 Dec. 2010.
4. *The Tony Evans Study Bible: Advancing God's Kingdom Agenda*. Holman Bible Publishers, 2017.
5. Hamilton, Victor P. *Handbook on the historical books: Joshua, Judges, Ruth, Samuel, Kings, Chronicles, Ezra-Nehemiah, Esther*. Grand Rapids, MI: Baker Academic, 2008, 187.
6. TheoWorkProject. "Tragedy Strikes the Family of Ruth and Naomi (Ruth 1:1-22)." Theology of Work. Accessed October 24, 2023.
7. Meyers, Carol. "Women and household maintenance, part I: Economic, reproductive, and sociopolitical activities." *Rediscovering Eve*, 27 Dec. 2012, pp. 125–146.
8. Ibid.
9. Ebeling, Jennie R. *Women's Lives in Biblical Times*. Bloomsbury Academic & Professional, 2010, 32.
10. Ibid.
11. Ibid.
12. Ebeling, Jennie R. *Women's Lives in Biblical Times*. Bloomsbury Academic & Professional, 2010, 30.
13. Summers, Juana, et al. "America Has a Loneliness Epidemic. Here Are 6 Steps to Address It." *NPR*, NPR, 2 May 2023, www.npr.org/2023/05/02/1173418268/loneliness-connection-mental-health-dementia-surgeon-general.
14. Walton, John H., Victor Harold Matthews, and Mark W. Chavalas. *The IVP Bible background: Old Testament*. Downers Grove, IL: InterVarsity Press, 2000, 281.
15. *New Bible Commentary*. Leicester, England: Copyright Universities and Colleges Christian Fellowship, 1994.

16. Ebeling, Jennie R. *Women's Lives in Biblical Times*. Bloomsbury Academic & Professional, 2010, 124.
17. Abasili, Alexander I. "Hannah's Ordeal of Childlessness: Interpreting 1 Samuel 1 through the Prism of a Childless African Woman in a Polygynous Family." *Old Testament Essays* 28, no. 3 (March 28, 2015): 581–605.
18. Ibid.
19. Tsumura, David Toshio. The First Book of Samuel. Grand Rapids, Mich: William B. Eerdmans, 2006;2007, 118.
20. Hertzberg, Hans Wilhelm. *I & II Samuel: a Commentary*. Philadelphia: Westminster Press, 1964, 25.
21. Abasili, Alexander I. "Hannah's ordeal of childlessness: Interpreting 1 samuel 1 through the prism of a childless African woman in a polygynous family." *Old Testament Essays*, vol. 28, no. 3, 2015, pp. 581–605.
22. Ibid.
23. Ibid.
24. Tsumura, David Toshio. The First Book of Samuel. Grand Rapids, Mich: William B. Eerdmans, 2006;2007, 118.
25. Ibid.
26. Abasili, Alexander I. "Hannah's Ordeal of Childlessness: Interpreting 1 Samuel 1 through the Prism of a Childless African Woman in a Polygynous Family." *Old Testament Essays* 28, no. 3 (March 28, 2015): 581–605.
27. Irene Nowell, OSB. "Women in the Old Testament." *Liturgical Press*, Liturgical Press, litpress.org/Products/E3886/Women-in-the-Old-Testament. Accessed 18 June 2024.
28. *New Bible Commentary*. Leicester, England: Copyright Universities and Colleges Christian Fellowship, 1994.
29. Barker, Kenneth L., et al. *The Expositor's Bible Commentary: Old Testament*. Zondervan Pub. House, Credo Reference, 2004, 382.
30. *New Bible Commentary*. Leicester, England: Copyright Universities and Colleges Christian Fellowship, 1994.
31. Ibid.
32. "Blue Letter Bible." *Blue Letter Bible*, www.blueletterbible.org/.
33. The Baker Illustrated Bible Commentary, edited by Gary M. Burge and Andrew E. Hill, Baker Books, 2012. ProQuest Ebook Central.
34. *New Bible Commentary*. Leicester, England: Copyright Universities and Colleges Christian Fellowship, 1994.
35. Ibid.
36. Ibid.
37. Ibid.

38. *NKJV: Spirit-filled life bible*. 3rd ed. Nashville, TN: Thomas Nelson, 2018, 364.
39. Ibid.
40. Adeyemo, Tokunboh. *Africa Bible Commentary*. Nairobi, Kenya: WordAlive Publishers, 2006.
41. Elwell, Walter A. *Evangelical dictionary of theology*. Grand Rapids: Baker Academic, 2001, 961.Hhh
42. Dharamraj, Havilah. *Ruth : A Pastoral and Contextual Commentary*. Carlisle: Langham Creative Projects, 2019. Accessed October 26, 2023. ProQuest Ebook Central.
43. Miller II, Robert D. "Orality and performance in ancient Israel." *Revue Des Sciences Religieuses*, no. 86/2, 15 Apr. 2012, pp. 183–194, https://doi.org/10.4000/rsr.1467.

Chapter 2: Jonah

1. Chisholm, Robert B. Handbook on the prophets: Isaiah, Jeremiah, Lamentations, Ezekiel, Daniel, Minor prophets. Grand Rapids, MI: Baker Academic, 2009, 409.
2. Swindoll, Chuck. Insight for Living Ministries. *https://insight.org/*. [Online] 2009. [Cited: January 22, 2024.
3. Bruckner, James K. Jonah, Nahum, Habakkuk, Zephaniah: The NIV Application Commentary from biblical text-- to contemporary life. Grand Rapids, MI: Zondervan, 2009.
4. Ibid.
5. Chisholm, Robert B. Handbook on the prophets: Isaiah, Jeremiah, Lamentations, Ezekiel, Daniel, Minor prophets. Grand Rapids, MI: Baker Academic, 2009, 409.
6. Alexander, T. Desmond, Baker, David W., Waltke, Bruce, and Desmond, Alexander T. Obadiah, Jonah and Micah. Downers Grove: Intervarsity Press, 2009, 86.
7. Ibid.
8. *ESV Study Bible: English Standard Version*. Crossway, 2008.
9. Jenson, Philip Peter. Obadiah, Jonah, Micah: a Theological Commentary. New York, NY: T&T Clark, 2008, 41.
10. Ibid.
11. Bruckner, James K. Jonah, Nahum, Habakkuk, Zephaniah: The NIV Application Commentary from biblical text-- to contemporary life. Grand Rapids, MI: Zondervan, 2009.
12. NKJV: Spirit-filled life bible. 3rd ed. Nashville, TN: Thomas Nelson, 2018.
13. Jenson, Philip Peter. Obadiah, Jonah, Micah: a Theological Commentary. New York, NY: T&T Clark, 2008, 41.
14. Ibid.

15. Mike Mills, October 9, 2019. "Historical and Cultural Background for Jonah." *Preaching Source*, preachingsource.com/blog/historical-and-cultural-background-for-jonah/. Accessed 18 June 2024.
16. Ibid.
17. Ibid.
18. NKJV: Spirit-filled life bible. 3rd ed. Nashville, TN: Thomas Nelson, 2018.
19. Ferreiro, Alberto, and Thomas C. Oden. The Twelve Prophets. Downers Grove, IL: InterVarsity Press, 2003, 130.
20. Mike Mills, October 9, 2019. "Historical and Cultural Background for Jonah." *Preaching Source*, preachingsource.com/blog/historical-and-cultural-background-for-jonah/. Accessed 18 June 2024.
21. Alexander, T. Desmond, Baker, David W., Waltke, Bruce, and Desmond, Alexander T. Obadiah, Jonah and Micah. Downers Grove: Intervarsity Press, 2009, 88.
22. Mike Mills, October 9, 2019. "Historical and Cultural Background for Jonah." *Preaching Source*, preachingsource.com/blog/historical-and-cultural-background-for-jonah/. Accessed 18 June 2024.
23. Ibid.
24. "Hamas's Murderous Attacks on Israel: CBN NewsWatch October 25, 2023." *CBN*, 25 Oct. 2023, www2.cbn.com/video/shows/hamass-murderous-attacks-israel-cbn-newswatch-october-25-2023.
25. NKJV: Spirit-filled life bible. 3rd ed. Nashville, TN: Thomas Nelson, 2018.
26. Mike Mills, October 9, 2019. "Historical and Cultural Background for Jonah." *Preaching Source*, preachingsource.com/blog/historical-and-cultural-background-for-jonah/. Accessed 18 June 2024.
27. NKJV: Spirit-filled life bible. 3rd ed. Nashville, TN: Thomas Nelson, 2018.
28. Ibid.
29. Alexander, T. Desmond, Baker, David W., Waltke, Bruce, and Desmond, Alexander T. Obadiah, Jonah and Micah. Downers Grove: Intervarsity Press, 2009, 93.
30. Ibid.
31. Ibid
32. Barker, Kenneth L., et al. *The Expositor's Bible Commentary: Old Testament*. Zondervan Pub. House, Credo Reference, 2004.
33. Barker, Kenneth L., et al. *The Expositor's Bible Commentary: Old Testament*. Zondervan Pub. House, Credo Reference, 2004.
34. Adeyemo, Tokunboh. *Africa Bible Commentary*. ABC Editorial Board, 2022.
35. Chisholm, Robert B. *Handbook on the prophets: Isaiah, Jeremiah, Lamentations, Ezekiel, Daniel, Minor prophets*. Grand Rapids, MI: Baker Academic, 2009, 411.

36. Carpenter, Eugene E., and Wayne McCown. *Asbury Bible Commentary*. Zondervan Pub. House, 1992.
37. Mike Mills, October 9, 2019. "Historical and Cultural Background for Jonah." *Preaching Source*, preachingsource.com/blog/historical-and-cultural-background-for-jonah/. Accessed 18 June 2024.
38. Carpenter, Eugene E., and Wayne McCown. *Asbury Bible Commentary*. Zondervan Pub. House, 1992.
39. Walton, John H., editor. *Zondervan Illustrated Bible Backgrounds Commentary Set: Old Testament*. Zondervan, 2009.
40. Ibid.
41. Ibid.
42. Ibid.
43. Carpenter, Eugene E., and Wayne McCown. *Asbury Bible Commentary*. Zondervan Pub. House, 1992.
44. Barker, Kenneth L., et al. *The Expositor's Bible Commentary: Old Testament*. Zondervan Pub. House, Credo Reference, 2004.
45. Adeyemo, Tokunboh. *Africa Bible Commentary*. ABC Editorial Board, 2022.
46. Mike Mills, October 9, 2019. "Historical and Cultural Background for Jonah." *Preaching Source*, preachingsource.com/blog/historical-and-cultural-background-for-jonah/. Accessed 18 June 2024.
47. "Olive Tree." *Olive Tree Bible Software*, www.olivetree.com/. Accessed 18 June 2024.
48. Ibid.
49. Ibid
50. Ferreiro, Alberto, and Thomas C. Oden. The Twelve Prophets. Downers Grove, IL: InterVarsity Press, 2003, 128.
51. Ibid.
52. "Jonah." *Book of Jonah Overview - Insight for Living Ministries*,
53. Ibid.

Chapter 3: Ruth

1. Barker, Kenneth L., and John R. Kohlenberger. The Expositor's Bible Commentary: Abridged edition. Grand Rapids, MI: Zondervan Pub. House, 2004.
2. McGee, J. Vernon. Thru the Bible - Genesis through Revelation. Nashville, TN: Thomas Nelson, 1981.
3. William A. Tooman. 2022. (Re)Reading Ruth. Eugene, Oregon: Cascade Books.

4. Barker, Kenneth L., and John R. Kohlenberger. The Expositor's Bible Commentary: Abridged edition. Grand Rapids, MI: Zondervan Pub. House, 2004.
5. Dharamraj, Havilah, and Philip Ewan Yalla. Ruth. Cumbria, UK: Langham Global Library, 2019.
6. McGee, J. Vernon. Thru the Bible - Genesis through Revelation. Nashville, TN: Thomas Nelson, 1981.
7. The Dictionary of Bible Themes, (London: Hodder & Stoughton, 2009), s.v. "Famine."
8. Dharamraj, Havilah, and Philip Ewan Yalla. Ruth. Cumbria, UK: Langham Global Library, 2019.
9. Mounce's Complete Expository Dictionary of Old & New Testament words, (Grand Rapids, MI: Zondervan, 2006), s.v. "Famine."
10. William A. Tooman. 2022. (Re)Reading Ruth. Eugene, Oregon: Cascade Books.
11. ESV Reformation Study Bible, Student Edition. Sanford, FL: Ligonier Ministries, 2021.
12. Hamilton, Victor P. Handbook on the historical books: Joshua, Judges, Ruth, Samuel, Kings, Chronicles, Ezra-Nehemiah, Esther. Grand Rapids, MI: Baker Academic, 2008, 190.
13. The Grace and Truth Study Bible. Grand Rapids, MI: Zondervan, 2021.
14. NIV, Cultural Backgrounds Study Bible. Grand Rapids, MI: Zondervan, 2016.
15. Barker, Kenneth L., and John R. Kohlenberger. The Expositor's Bible Commentary: Abridged edition. Grand Rapids, MI: Zondervan Pub. House, 2004.
16. Ibid.
17. Dharamraj, Havilah, and Philip Ewan Yalla. Ruth. Cumbria, UK: Langham Global Library, 2019.
18. NIV first-century study Bible: Explore scripture in its Jewish and early Christian context. Grand Rapids, MI: Zondervan, 2014.
19. Walton, John H., Victor Harold Matthews, and Mark W. Chavalas. The IVP Bible background: Old Testament. Downers Grove, IL: InterVarsity Press, 2000, 277.
20. Bolen, Todd. "The Widow in Ancient Society." BiblePlaces.com. Accessed October 25, 2023. https://www.bibleplaces.com/blog/author/tbolen/.
21. Walton, John H., Victor Harold Matthews, and Mark W. Chavalas. The IVP Bible background: Old Testament. Downers Grove, IL: InterVarsity Press, 2000, 277.
22. Dharamraj, Havilah, and Philip Ewan Yalla. Ruth. Cumbria, UK: Langham Global Library, 2019.
23. Bolen, Todd. "The Widow in Ancient Society." BiblePlaces.com. Accessed October 25, 2023.
24. Dharamraj, Havilah, and Philip Ewan Yalla. Ruth. Cumbria, UK: Langham Global Library, 2019.

25. Barker, Kenneth L., et al. *The Expositor's Bible Commentary: Old Testament*. Zondervan Pub. House, Credo Reference, 2004.
26. Ibid.
27. Adeyemo, Tokunboh. *Africa Bible Commentary*. ABC Editorial Board, 2022.
28. William A. Tooman. 2022. (Re)Reading Ruth. Eugene, Oregon: Cascade Books.
29. Ibid.
30. "H4755 - mārā' - Strong's Hebrew Lexicon (kjv)." Blue Letter Bible. Accessed 26 Oct, 2023.
31. "H5281 - nāʿŏmî - Strong's Hebrew Lexicon (kjv)." Blue Letter Bible. Accessed 26 Oct, 2023.
32. Barker, Kenneth L., and John R. Kohlenberger. The Expositor's Bible Commentary: Abridged edition. Grand Rapids, MI: Zondervan Pub. House, 2004.
33. Ibid.
34. Ibid.
35. Ibid
36. *ESV Study Bible: English Standard Version*. Crossway, 2008.
37. Barker, Kenneth L., and John R. Kohlenberger. The Expositor's Bible Commentary: Abridged edition. Grand Rapids, MI: Zondervan Pub. House, 2004.
38. "Blue Letter Bible." *Blue Letter Bible*, www.blueletterbible.org/
39. Strong, James. *The New Strong's Expanded Exhaustive Concordance of the Bible*. Thomas Nelson, 2010.
40. "Blue Letter Bible." *Blue Letter Bible*, www.blueletterbible.org/
41. Strong, James. *The New Strong's Expanded Exhaustive Concordance of the Bible*. Thomas Nelson, 2010.
42. Barker, Kenneth L., et al. *The Expositor's Bible Commentary: Old Testament*. Zondervan Pub. House, Credo Reference, 2004.
43. Rothstein, Rabbi Isaiah. "The Power of Jewish Blessings." *My Jewish Learning*, 7 Feb. 2019, www.myjewishlearning.com/article/blessings-a-conduit-of-infinite-potential/.
44. Barker, Kenneth L., and John R. Kohlenberger. The Expositor's Bible Commentary: Abridged edition. Grand Rapids, MI: Zondervan Pub. House, 2004.

Made in the USA
Columbia, SC
14 November 2024